THE GREAT GROMBOOLIAN PLAIN

AND OTHER PLAYS

by

Don Nigro

SAMUEL FRENCH, INC.

45 WEST 25TH STREET   NEW YORK 10010

7623 SUNSET BOULEVARD   HOLLYWOOD 90046

LONDON   *TORONTO*

IMPORTANT BILLING AND CREDIT REQUIREMENTS

All producers of THE GREAT GROMBOOLIAN PLAIN AND OTHER PLAYS *must* give credit to the Author of the Play in all programs distributed in connection with performances of the Play and in all instances in which the title of the Play appears for purposes of advertising, publicizing or otherwise exploiting the Play and/or a production. The name of the Author *must* also appear on a separate line, on which no other name appears, immediately following the title, and *must* appear in size of type not less than fifty percent the size of the title type.

CONTENTS

THE GREAT GROMBOOLIAN PLAIN

And often since, in the nights of June
we sit on the sand and watch the moon.
She has gone to the great Gromboolian plain,
and we probably never shall meet again.

Oft, in the long, still nights of June,
we sit on the rocks and watch the moon.
She dwells by the streams of the Chankly Bore,
and we probably never shall see her more.

—Edward Lear, *"The Pelican Chorus"*

CHARACTERS:

DINAH, a young woman in her early twenties
NURSE, a young woman in her twenties
YOUNG MAN, in his twenties
MAGELLAN, a man in his late thirties
APRIL, a young woman in her late twenties

SETTING:

Two benches amid greenery.

THE GREAT GROMBOOLIAN PLAIN was first presented in April of 1998 by the Shadowbox Cabaret in Columbus, Ohio with the following cast:

Dinah ....Colleen Dalton
Nurse ....Carrie Lynn McDonald
Young Man ....Mark Slack
Magellan ....Steven Guyer
April ....Rebecca Gentile

It was directed by Julie Klein.
Assistant Director was Tom Cardinal.

THE GREAT GROMBOOLIAN PLAIN

(In the darkness, the sound of carousel music, an old fashioned orchestrion version of "The Band Played On." Lights up slowly, flickering lights as in an old movie. DINAH, a young woman in her early twenties, sits on a bench amid greenery. A young man is sitting on a nearby bench. A nurse, a young woman in her twenties, is wheeling an old fashioned baby carriage into view. DINAH is dressed in modern clothing, but the Nurse and the Young Man are both dressed in the style of the 1890s. The Young Man seems mesmerized by the Nurse, who is fussing with the baby and appears not to notice. She drops a small stuffed animal. The Young Man looks at it, hesitates. Dinah is watching them with great interest. Then the flickering lights begin to darken, and the Nurse and the Young Man begin to fade slowly and drift out of sight as lights come up more brightly on Dinah, no more flickering effect. Sound of birds. A summer day. MAGELLAN, a man in his late thirties, dressed in modern clothing, enters, sits on the bench vacated by the Young Man, and begins to read a book. DINAH watches him for a bit.)

DINAH. So what are you in for?
MAGELLAN. Pardon?
DINAH. What's your particular brand of socially unacceptable behavior? They take all kinds here, as long as you've got the money.

MAGELLAN. Yes, I'm sure they do.

DINAH. You don't look rich. Ordinarily you've got to be rich to be crazy in this place. You look too real to be rich. Are you a homicidal maniac?

MAGELLAN. Do I look like a homicidal maniac?

DINAH. You look like a man with a secret.

MAGELLAN. What are you in for?

DINAH. What do you think?

MAGELLAN. You believe you're Napoleon's horse?

DINAH. No. That was last year. I'm over that now. Except once in a while I get this terrible craving for oats. It comes and goes. Guess again.

MAGELLAN. You believe that circus animals live in your underwear.

DINAH. No, but you're getting warmer.

MAGELLAN. I give up. What?

DINAH. If I tell you, you'll think I'm crazy.

MAGELLAN. Well, of course you're crazy. You wouldn't be here if you weren't crazy. You'd have to be crazy to be spending this kind of money if you weren't crazy. The question we're addressing ourselves to at the moment is, just what particular flavor of crazy are you?

DINAH. Then you're admitting that you're crazy?

MAGELLAN. I did something crazy.

DINAH. Just one thing?

MAGELLAN. Well, two things, really. I married my wife.

DINAH. That's pretty crazy. The one person you should never marry is your wife.

MAGELLAN. And then I tried to strangle her.

DINAH. So you ARE a homicidal maniac.

MAGELLAN. Not a very successful one, I'm afraid. Just a man with a short fuse and an unfortunate wife.

DINAH. So she's not dead?

MAGELLAN. Not from the neck down. No, she's all right.

DINAH. And you pleaded temporary insanity?

MAGELLAN. Something like that.

DINAH. So where is she now?

MAGELLAN. In Acapulco with a Brazilian nut farmer, having the time of her life on a nude beach. And I'm here with you, on our own little nut farm. Funny how things work out.

DINAH. Poetic justice, kind of. Except we're not naked. Well, not yet, anyway. My name's Dinah. As in the person someone's in the kitchen with, in the old song. Strumming on the old banjo. You know that one? I guess not. What's your name?

MAGELLAN. Does it matter?

DINAH. Don't you want to give out that information to other crazy people?

MAGELLAN. Not particularly, no.

DINAH. That's not very friendly of you.

MAGELLAN. I'm not a very friendly guy. And I think you'll find, as you grow older, Dinah, and spend more time out of the kitchen, and away from your banjo, that a rather large percentage of men who attempt to strangle their wives are not particularly friendly people.

DINAH. Actually, you're name's Magellan. I love your name. It's beautiful.

MAGELLAN. How did you know my name?

DINAH. I help out in the office sometimes. It's therapy for me. I like to snoop through the files of the new people, and I thought your picture was kind of cute, or at least different, so I took a peek at your records, and I've been watching you ever since. You're not like the other people here.

MAGELLAN. I'm not?

DINAH. No. You're much more, I don't know, self-possessed.

MAGELLAN. If you looked at my file, then you already knew about my wife, so why did you ask me?

DINAH. I wanted to see if you'd lie about it. I like to know early on in a relationship if I can trust people or not. I have a tendency to be a little too trustful for my own good, which is something I've been trying to cure lately by becoming really paranoid.

MAGELLAN. I see. And what else did you find out about me?

DINAH. That's about it. The nurse came back from sneaking her cigarette in the laundry room and I almost got caught. It's such a wonderful name, Magellan. You circumnavigated the earth, you know.

MAGELLAN. Not me.

DINAH. And the Magellanic Clouds were named after you.

MAGELLAN. I'm afraid that was before my time.

DINAH. No it wasn't. Nothing is before anybody's time. And nothing is after anybody's time.

MAGELLAN. What does that mean?

DINAH. That's what I'm in for. I'm a time traveller.

MAGELLAN. A time traveller?

DINAH. Yes.

MAGELLAN. Oh.

DINAH. No, really. I am.

MAGELLAN. You travel in time?

DINAH. Absolutely.

MAGELLAN. Well, good.

DINAH. You think that sounds crazy, don't you?

MAGELLAN. I'm not exactly in any position to pass judgment about that, am I?

DINAH. I really do. It's a gift. My sister is desperately jealous of my time travelling abilities. She's the one who put me in here.

MAGELLAN. Because she's jealous?

DINAH. That, and because she wants me to tell her something that I won't tell her, so she got me thrown in the booby hatch until I give in.

MAGELLAN. What does she want to know?

DINAH. That's a secret.

MAGELLAN. Ah. Okay. So where do you go when you travel in time? Last week? Tomorrow?

DINAH. Any place I want to.

MAGELLAN. Do you have a time machine hidden in the

bushes, or what?

DINAH. I don't need a machine.

MAGELLAN. H.G. Wells needed a machine.

DINAH. No he didn't. His character did. All he needed was his brain.

MAGELLAN. So, in other words, you just imagine that you're travelling to other times.

DINAH. No. I go there.

MAGELLAN. Uh huh.

DINAH. Don't look at me like I'm crazy.

MAGELLAN. Well, you ARE here in what you've just referred to with great sensitivity as the booby hatch.

DINAH. You're in the booby hatch, and you're not crazy.

MAGELLAN. You'd prefer to think of me as a more or less sane but somewhat incompetent would-be murderer, would you?

DINAH. I travel in time. What do I care if you believe me or not? You beat your wife.

MAGELLAN. I didn't beat my wife, I tried to strangle my wife. It's an entirely different thing. I would never beat my wife. I never hit her once, at any time. I just put my hands around her throat and squeezed for a while.

DINAH. And then what?

MAGELLAN. And then I stopped.

DINAH. So you didn't really want to kill her?

MAGELLAN. Maybe just for a second or two.

DINAH. Why?

MAGELLAN. It's a secret.

DINAH. Screwed around on you, didn't she?

MAGELLAN. She was unfaithful, yes.

DINAH. If you really loved her, you'd forgive her.

MAGELLAN. She was unfaithful with half the population of Connecticut.

DINAH. Well, that's not good. There's a lot of people in Connecticut.

MAGELLAN. So I took up drinking, but that didn't really

make me feel a whole lot better, so I tried to strangle her instead.

DINAH. Did that make you feel better?

MAGELLAN. No.

DINAH. And here you are.

MAGELLAN. And here I am.

DINAH. What do you do when you're not strangling your wife?

MAGELLAN. I'm a Park Ranger.

DINAH. No you're not.

MAGELLAN. It's true, I swear. Have I ever lied to you?

DINAH. Do you live in the woods and eat berries and fruit?

MAGELLAN. Not exactly.

DINAH. And your wife didn't appreciate this rustic life?

MAGELLAN. She thought she would. But she didn't. I met her in college. I was studying trees and trying to write. She liked that. She had this beautiful fantasy of us living in the woods together. I'd go out to protect the squirrels each day and she'd stay home in the cabin and photograph fruit or something.

DINAH. Well, that sounds nice.

MAGELLAN. It sounded pretty good to me, too. But it didn't work. She started to go crazy up there.

DINAH. She goes crazy and they lock you up. Funny world.

MAGELLAN. She got a place in town, just for occasional use, until I paid her a surprise visit one night and discovered just what she was using it for. She swore it would never happen again and I forgave her, sort of. Then it happened again and I started strangling her. And the rest is history. Except for you time travellers, of course. For you, I guess the past is always the present, at least potentially.

DINAH. The past always was the present. So what did you write?

MAGELLAN. Nothing much. Quite a lot, actually. But nothing much.

DINAH. My father was a writer.

MAGELLAN. Really? Let me guess. Shakespeare?

DINAH. No, Spenser.

MAGELLAN. Oh. Well, I had the right historical period, anyway.

DINAH. No, not Edmund Spenser, stupid. John James Spenser. Haven't you heard of him?

MAGELLAN. I don't think so.

DINAH. He won the Pulitzer Prize.

MAGELLAN. I'm sure he did.

DINAH. Don't patronize me. My father was John James Spenser and he won the Pulitzer Prize. You can look it up in your Funk and Wagnalls.

MAGELLAN. Okay. Okay. You don't have to get testy about it.

DINAH. You can't be much of a writer if you never heard of my father. He was a great poet.

MAGELLAN. I'm not much up on modern poetry. I wrote about nature.

DINAH. My father wrote about nature. And time. He was fascinated by time. And women. A lot about women.

MAGELLAN. Did your father also win the Nobel Prize?

DINAH. No. Just the Pulitzer.

MAGELLAN. Why not? What's the matter with him?

DINAH. Nothing's the matter with him. He died.

MAGELLAN. Oh. A great loss to world literature.

DINAH. A great loss to me.

(Pause. DINAH sits there. MAGELLAN looks at her.)

MAGELLAN. I'm sorry. I thought you were joking. Or crazy. Or both. I mean, when you jump right from time travel to the Pulitzer Prize, I guess I have a little trouble separating fantasy from reality.

DINAH. Maybe that's why you're here.

MAGELLAN. Could be. *(Pause.)* When did your father die?

DINAH. Last year.

MAGELLAN. How long have you been here?

DINAH. A couple of months. My sister did it.

MAGELLAN. Your sister did what? Killed your father?

DINAH. No. Put me in here. She hates me.

MAGELLAN. I don't think she hates you.

DINAH. What the hell would you know about it?

MAGELLAN. Nothing at all, really, I just—

DINAH. Then shut up. She's a model, with an extremely high IQ and no brain whatsoever. Maybe you'd like to strangle her for me some time.

MAGELLAN. Why are you so mad at your sister?

DINAH. Wouldn't you be a little annoyed if somebody had you kidnapped and stuck in the booby hatch?

MAGELLAN. Somebody did stick me in the booby hatch.

DINAH. Yes, but your alternative was probably hard time in the slammer.

MAGELLAN. This is true. Look, she must have thought she had a good reason to put you in here.

DINAH. Yes, she had a good reason, but it didn't have anything to do with time travel.

MAGELLAN. What was it, then?

DINAH. None of your business.

MAGELLAN. Fine. I just thought that, since I gave you a lurid, blow by blow account of my efforts to asphyxiate my unfaithful wife, you might want to volunteer a little something about yourself. I haven't had the advantage of snooping in your file.

DINAH. She put me in here because I know where our father's last book is, and I won't tell her.

MAGELLAN. She put you in here over a book?

DINAH. He finished it just before he died. I found the manuscript in his desk. And then I hid it so she wouldn't find it.

MAGELLAN. Why did you do that?

DINAH. Because I didn't want her to get her hands on it.

MAGELLAN. Why not?

DINAH. She just wants it so she can publish it.

MAGELLAN. And you don't want it published?

DINAH. No.

MAGELLAN. I don't understand. I mean, if it's your father's last book—

DINAH. She thinks I want to keep it for myself. She thinks I don't want her to have any of the money.

MAGELLAN. Do you?

DINAH. No book of poems is going to make anybody rich.

MAGELLAN. But she doesn't know that?

DINAH. Of course she knows it. But it isn't really about money. It's more about control. She wants to be in control of everything, you know?

MAGELLAN. So she put you in here until you tell her where the manuscript is, is that right?

DINAH. That's it.

MAGELLAN. Why don't you just tell her where it is, and get it published, and split the profits?

DINAH. I can't talk to you any more today. I've got to be someplace now.

MAGELLAN. Got an appointment with Dr. Noff? What a great guy. Looks like an ax murderer to me.

DINAH. No. I won't talk to that guy. He gives me the creeps.

MAGELLAN. Well then, where are you going? I mean, this place has got a big wall around it. What are you going to do? Go time travelling?

DINAH. What if I am?

MAGELLAN. I don't mean to pry, it's just, I'm kind of interested in how you do that.

DINAH. Why?

MAGELLAN. I don't know. What else have I got to do? I've never met a time traveller before. Do you visit famous historical moments?

DINAH. Oh, God, no. They're usually violent and ugly, or boring, or both. I prefer quiet places. Obscure little corners of time. In my time travel I try to seek out the most peaceful and forgotten little lost parts of eternity. Places I can go when I get angry or depressed.

MAGELLAN. Do you disappear when you time travel?

DINAH. No. You do it with your mind. Your mind goes and lives temporarily in another time. I don't know exactly how it happens. I just know I can do it. You can see and hear and feel and smell everything there, but the people in the time you visit don't usually seem to notice that you're there, if you don't stay too long. After a while I think they start to get a funny feeling somebody is watching them. I think the longer you stay, the more real you become. If you stayed a long time, you might get trapped there, be like real flesh and blood there. Time seems to want to pull you into wherever you are and make you real there. That's why a time traveller needs to learn when to leave.

MAGELLAN. What happens if some day you travel to some place in time and get trapped there, and can't get back?

DINAH. Then my sister will be very happy.

MAGELLAN. Do you visit the future, too?

DINAH. When I was a little girl I did, sometimes, but it's a lot harder, and it really scared me, because it hadn't happened yet, so I don't go there much any more.

MAGELLAN. What's the future like?

DINAH. I don't know. I prefer the past.

MAGELLAN. So you can pretty much control exactly where and when you go, just by willing it?

DINAH. Not exactly. I mean, it isn't exactly willing, so much as allowing, and sometimes you can get pulled someplace you didn't want to go at all. It's like these waves of time or consciousness or emotion or something, like wind, you know? It's like being a leaf in November. Sometimes it wants to blow you in one direction or another, but if you know how to ride the wind currents, you can go exploring more or less wherever you want to.

MAGELLAN. Sounds wonderful.

DINAH. It is, mostly. But sometimes it isn't. Sometimes it scares me.

MAGELLAN. When did you first discover you could do this?

DINAH. It was at my mother's funeral. I wanted so badly to be someplace else, never in my life had I wanted so desperately not to be where I was, it was so awful. And I guess I wanted to go away so much that it somehow tripped off the time travel mechanism in my brain, because I'd just been reading Sherlock Holmes stories, and suddenly I was there. In London. I don't mean that I was daydreaming. I was really there, standing on this foggy street at night, and there was this carriage going by, and I saw this thick, strong man with a big mustache walking by in the fog. It was Sir Arthur Conan Doyle, probably walking home to write down another Sherlock Holmes story. I was there in the fog with Sir Arthur Conan Doyle, one night in the 1890s in London, a very ordinary foggy night, nothing special about it except that I was there, and it was amazing. And I felt so close to him, and to the people we passed on the street. I think time travel requires a great capacity to connect emotionally with another person in another time and place. It's sort of like love. Time travel is like love. Only not so messy.

MAGELLAN. You were in love with Sir Arthur Conan Doyle?

DINAH. No, not in love, just—oh, it's so hard to explain. It's like having a dream that you're someplace else, only all the time you're still perfectly aware that you're you, and even that you're dreaming, like reading a very good book, that sort of really vivid, completely engrossing dream. Only it isn't a dream. It's time travel. And that's what I do. I guess it's a way of escaping, only something always brings me back here. To me, to this body, this time and place. I don't know, maybe it's some sort of rule, that while time itself seems to want to keep you wherever you happen to land in it, the time traveller feels this very strong need to be able to return to her point of departure, like the murderer to the scene of the crime. It's like reality is this uneasy equilibrium between where you want to be and where you are. You think this is all one big crock of shit, don't you?

MAGELLAN. I didn't say that.

DINAH. You're just like the doctors here, that sadistic, patronizing, narcissistic pack of chain smoking degenerates. Every one of them is certifiable, and they're telling me I'm crazy.

MAGELLAN. Give me a chance. I just met you. Can't I have a minute or two to absorb this new view of the universe you're offering here?

DINAH. Don't humor me, all right? I don't need to be humored.

MAGELLAN. I'm not humoring you.

DINAH. You people go around looking so smug and feeling so damned superior—

MAGELLAN. What people? What category have you just stuck me in? Don't put me in with the doctors, I'll lose my mind.

DINAH. You people who think you know all the answers. I know you. The conspiracy of the allegedly sane, the smug fraternity of mediocrity that runs the world and spends most of its time trying to kill the people who actually use their brains once in a while.

MAGELLAN. Wait a minute. I don't run anything. You don't know me at all.

DINAH. Yes I do.

MAGELLAN. No you don't. You don't know anything about me but what I've told you, and what you read in my files, which were made up by those doctors you have such respect for. I could be anybody. You have secret places, I have secret places. You don't know about mine, and I don't know about yours, so stop trying to stuff me into some kind of goddamn coffin of preconceived character traits so you don't have to think about me any more.

DINAH. Why should I want to think about you any more?

MAGELLAN. I don't know. And I don't really care a whole hell of a lot, either.

DINAH. So why are you talking to me then?

MAGELLAN. You're the one who struck up this conversation, not me. You thought I was cute, remember?

DINAH. Well, I was wrong about that. So what are you going to do? Strangle me?

MAGELLAN. No, I only strangle women I'm in love with.

DINAH. Well, fine. I'm leaving now.

MAGELLAN. What's the matter? Is this starting to feel too real? You afraid you're going to get trapped in this particular time and place? Running off to the French Revolution, to have a conversation with Marie Antoinette's head?

DINAH. No, I'm going inside to talk to my friend Lucille, who thinks she's a submarine.

MAGELLAN. Great. Have a nice trip. Just remember not to come up too quickly afterwards, or you'll get the bends.

DINAH. I'll try to keep that in mind.

(DINAH starts to go.)

MAGELLAN. Wait a minute.

DINAH. What?

MAGELLAN. How does a person learn to do this time travel thing? Can it be taught?

DINAH. How should I know?

MAGELLAN. I thought you were the world's greatest authority on this.

DINAH. Why do you care?

MAGELLAN. I thought it might come in handy some day. Well, it sounds better than sitting around here on the funny farm for the next five to fifteen years of my life. Actually, time travel is looking pretty good to me at the moment. What's the matter? Don't you want to share your big discovery? You want to keep it all to yourself?

DINAH. I'm not sure it can be taught. I never tried to teach anybody. You're the first person who ever believed me before. Except that you don't really believe me either. You probably just want to get into my underpants.

MAGELLAN. No I don't.

DINAH. Sure. Right. Nice try, Bozo. You know, if I start screaming and say you tried to molest me, they'll probably move you to a zoo for the criminally insane.

MAGELLAN. Okay. That's it for me. Sorry I bothered you.

DINAH. Wait a minute.

MAGELLAN. What?

DINAH. I didn't say I wanted you to leave. I just don't want you to be humoring me. I don't like ulterior motives. My tendency to trust people gets me into trouble. That's why I don't trust people.

MAGELLAN. Well, that makes sense.

DINAH. Not really.

MAGELLAN. So how do I travel in time?

DINAH. You really want to try it?

MAGELLAN. Yes. I do. Teach me.

DINAH. You promise, you swear on your children's grave that your motives are pure here? That you sincerely want to know how to do this? You swear?

(MAGELLAN looks at DINAH, starts to answer, then stops. Then APRIL appears, an attractive young woman in her late twenties.)

APRIL. There you are.

DINAH. Oh, great.

APRIL. I don't want to interrupt, if you're busy doing something.

DINAH. No, it's all right, this guy was just trying to worm his way into my underpants.

APRIL. Well, I can wait over here until you're done. I was just—

DINAH. Snooping around like a weasel?

APRIL. I wasn't snooping around. I came to see you. Is that a crime?

DINAH. Well, here I am. Now you've seen me, you can die happy.

APRIL. How are you, Dinah?

DINAH. I'm insane, thank you. How are you? Never mind. We don't really care. Magellan, this is my sister April. She makes her living wearing almost nothing or stupid overpriced crap for phoney people with no brains. And this is my friend, Magellan. He circumnavigated the globe, has big clouds of gas in space named after him, and he strangled his wife.

MAGELLAN. I'm very pleased to meet you, April.

(MAGELLAN holds out his hand. APRIL hesitates.)

DINAH. Don't worry. He only strangles women he's in love with.

MAGELLAN. Maybe I should go away so you two can talk.

DINAH. Oh, don't go. I'm sure April would love to hear all about your unsuccessful murder attempt on your wife.

APRIL. I would like to speak with my sister for just a bit, if you don't mind, Mr.—

MAGELLAN. Magellan. No, I don't mind.

DINAH. Yes he does. He was just about to get into my underpants.

MAGELLAN. That's okay. I'll just go over to the gazebo and look up Lucille's periscope or something. Another time, maybe?

DINAH. Another time. Sure. *(MAGELLAN looks at DINAH, then at APRIL, then goes.)* So, is this your weekly appeal to reason?

APRIL. I come to see you every week because I care about you.

DINAH. Is that why you stuck me in here? Because you care about me?

APRIL. Yes, as a matter of fact, it is.

DINAH. You don't lie very well, April. But then, you don't do anything very well but sit and look pretty, do you? What a waste of all those extra IQ points.

APRIL. Dinah, I want you to get well. I know you think I just put you in here because I want Daddy's book, but that's not true.

DINAH. You don't want Daddy's book?

APRIL. I do want Daddy's book, but that's not why I put you in here.

DINAH. You mean if I tell you where it is, you still won't let me out? That doesn't provide me with a whole lot of incentive here, now, does it? Think, April, think. Use that big fat brain of yours. I can't remember you using it for anything important since you taught me how to subtract.

APRIL. If you did tell me where the book is, it would show that you're not quite as disturbed a person as you were when you hid it from me.

DINAH. I am not a disturbed person. You are a disturbed person. I am a prisoner in a country club for rich people's crazy relatives.

APRIL. If you weren't a disturbed person you never would have hidden it in the first place. Why don't you just let me have it, so we can get it published? You know that's what Daddy would have wanted.

DINAH. You don't know that. You haven't even read it.

APRIL. How can I read it if you won't tell me where it is? We owe it to him, Dinah.

DINAH. You don't owe him anything.

APRIL. How can you say that?

DINAH. I can say anything I want to. I'm a lunatic.

APRIL. Have you read it?

DINAH. So, how's your life going? Still sleeping with that half-wit who does metal sculptures of dancing cigarettes?

APRIL. No.

DINAH. Oh, that's too bad. I thought you two were perfect

for each other.

APRIL. You seem to have made a friend.

DINAH. Yeah, right. He thinks I'm crazy.

APRIL. Well, you ARE crazy, and apparently so is he, so at least you have something in common.

DINAH. If you just came here to tell me I'm crazy, you're wasting your time. I mean, you're paying good money to bad doctors to do that. So why don't you just go away and work on your pouting and strutting or whatever the hell you do when you're not being a photographer's zombie and leave me alone, all right?

APRIL. I miss you.

DINAH. Sure you do.

APRIL. I do. I really do. Why don't you believe me? Do you know how much money I could be making in Europe now?

DINAH. Well, go, then. I'm not stopping you.

APRIL. I can't go to Europe and leave you in here.

DINAH. Then get me the hell out of this place.

APRIL. I can't do that. You need help.

DINAH. I need a better sister, is what I need.

APRIL. Why do you hate me so much?

DINAH. Gee, I don't know, April. You don't suppose it might have something to do with you having me dragged off and locked up in a mental institution, do you?

APRIL. Dinah, you believe you take vacations in the nineteenth century.

DINAH. And you believe you put me in here because you love me, so I guess we're both suffering from pretty severe delusions, huh?

APRIL. You think you can finally own Daddy, now that he's dead, don't you?

DINAH. I don't want to own him.

APRIL. Then why did you hide his book?

DINAH. I'm sorry, I've got to run, I think it's time for my shock treatments. Don't hang around here too long, honey, or

they'll mistake you for one of the lobotomy patients.
    APRIL. Dinah. Wait. Dinah.

(But DINAH is gone. APRIL sits down on the bench and holds her head. A moment. Just the sound of the birds. Then MAGELLAN returns.)

    MAGELLAN. You know, you'd do a lot better with her if you didn't go right to the screaming.
    APRIL. Get away from me.
    MAGELLAN. It's all right. She went back into the building. Are you crying?
    APRIL. No. Go away.
    MAGELLAN. Do you need a handkerchief?
    APRIL. Don't fuss at me. I hate being fussed at. I'm not paying you to fuss at me.
    MAGELLAN. All right, all right, just relax.
    APRIL. And don't tell me to relax.
    MAGELLAN. Okay. Throw a fit if you like. Hell, this is certainly the place for it.
    APRIL. What did you find out?
    MAGELLAN. We're just getting acquainted.
    APRIL. What the hell are you waiting for?
    MAGELLAN. I had to let her find me. I couldn't be coming at her, or she'd be suspicious. She's not stupid, you know.
    APRIL. So she hasn't told you anything?
    MAGELLAN. Well, I'm learning a great deal about time travel.
    APRIL. I don't want to hear about her stupid time travel fantasies. I want to know where my father's manuscript is. Didn't she say anything about it?
    MAGELLAN. She talked about it a little. I can't be pumping her for information, it's got to come out of her naturally. I think she'll tell me, eventually. She's pretty desperate for somebody to talk to, but she's got to trust me first, and that's going to take a little time.

APRIL. Great. And while she's learning to trust you, I'm paying for two people to stay here. Do you know how much this place costs?

MAGELLAN. I thought this wasn't about money.

APRIL. It's not about money. She'll get half the money. The book belongs to both of us. All Daddy's copyrights do.

MAGELLAN. But if she stays in here, you pretty much get control of everything, don't you?

APRIL. I don't want her money. I've already spent a lot more money keeping her in this place than we'll ever see from royalties on any damned book of poetry. If it is poetry. I don't even know what it is. I haven't seen it. Why won't she let me see it? And that was a real inspiration telling her you're in here for trying to murder your wife. Boy, that's going to get her to trust you.

MAGELLAN. Don't tell me my business, all right? If you want my advice, just let it go, and get her out of here. She doesn't belong in this place.

APRIL. You don't think she's crazy?

MAGELLAN. Everybody is crazy. I don't think she's going to do any harm to herself or anybody else.

APRIL. I'm not paying you to give me advice. Just find out where the book is.

MAGELLAN. And then you'll get her out of here, if I do, right? You will get her out of here?

APRIL. What business is that of yours?

MAGELLAN. I'm just not entirely comfortable about messing about in somebody's life like this.

APRIL. That's your job, Magellan. Your ex-wife said you were good at this sort of thing.

MAGELLAN. Well, that was big of her.

APRIL. She said it was the only thing you're good at.

MAGELLAN. Yes, that sounds more like her. I am good at this. I'm very good at this. But philandering husbands and long lost relatives are one thing. This is something else. This is— this is a nice person here. A very strange person, maybe, but a—I don't want to do anything bad to this person.

APRIL. And you think I do?

MAGELLAN. I don't know.

APRIL. She's my sister. I just want the manuscript so we can get it published and be done with it. I just want to do that for our father. I know that's what he would have wanted. And she won't let me. It's spite, that's all it is. It's entirely out of cold, terrible, vicious spite. She's always been a selfish little brat, always jealous of me, of how close I was with our father. She's always had contempt for what I do. I'm afraid she'll destroy it. I mean, she could do anything, she's away in her own private fantasy world half the time. If she gets out of here before I can get my hands on that manuscript, I really think she might burn it.

MAGELLAN. She loved your father, didn't she? So why would she burn his last book?

APRIL. I don't know what she'd do. You've talked to her. How can I trust a person who seriously believes she can travel in time?

MAGELLAN. Was she always this way? She says she started doing this when she was a little girl, at your mother's funeral.

APRIL. At first I think it was a kind of game she would play, it was a way of dealing with the pain, of getting away from it for a while, like reading a book or seeing a movie or something. I thought she'd outgrow it. But apparently she never did. Or the shock of our father's death has brought it back, made her retreat into that imaginary world again. That's what the doctors think. I don't want to hurt her, I would never do her any harm or willingly cause her any unhappiness, I swear, I've just got to find that manuscript so I know it's safe, and get it into print. It would have meant so much to our father. She'll be proud of it when it's published. She just, I don't know, maybe it's like the last part of Daddy she can keep all to herself, and she can't bear to share it with me. Will you just find out where it is for me? Please?

MAGELLAN. I'll do the best I can.

APRIL. Thank you.

MAGELLAN. Don't thank me. You're paying me very well, and I get free meals here, and all the medication I want, and I just met a woman who thinks she's a submarine. What more could I ask? Anyway, I like the fringe benefits.

APRIL. Well, you'd better.

(APRIL kisses MAGELLAN, a long, tender kiss.)

MAGELLAN. What else did my ex-wife tell you about me?

APRIL. She said she thought you'd fit right in here.

MAGELLAN. Sweet girl.

APRIL. And she warned me not to get involved with you.

MAGELLAN. Good advice.

APRIL. Too late. Well, I've got to go. Good luck.

MAGELLAN. Yeah. *(APRIL starts away, then turns back.)* What?

APRIL. Be careful with her, okay? I mean, she's just a kid. In her mind, especially. I don't want her to get messed up any further than she already is by this.

MAGELLAN. I'll be careful. I promise.

APRIL. Okay.

(APRIL looks at MAGELLAN for a moment. Then she goes. MAGELLAN sits down on the bench, troubled. Bird sounds. Then DINAH appears behind him.)

DINAH. You were talking to her.

MAGELLAN. *(Startled, jumping like a guilty thing.)* What? Who?

DINAH. You were talking to my sister. I saw you.

MAGELLAN. Yes. I was.

DINAH. What about?

MAGELLAN. About you.

DINAH. What was she saying about me?

MAGELLAN. That she loves you, and she's worried about you.

DINAH. Why would she talk to you about me? She doesn't even know you, does she?

MAGELLAN. She seemed to be trying to pump me for information. She wanted to know if you'd talked to me about your father's book.

DINAH. And what did you tell her?

MAGELLAN. I described to her in great detail the extreme pleasure it gave me to strangle my wife. I was just getting to the good part when she remembered she had to be some place else.

DINAH. Did she try to bribe you?

MAGELLAN. No. Actually, she seemed pretty sincere to me. I mean, sincerely concerned about you.

DINAH. Then why did you scare her away?

MAGELLAN. I don't like betrayal. I don't like being part of it. I mean, at the moment, you and Lucille are the only friends I've got, and Lucille keeps submerging on me. Besides, I want to learn how to do this time travel thing.

DINAH. No you don't.

MAGELLAN. Yes I do. Really.

DINAH. There's things about it I haven't told you.

MAGELLAN. What? Do I have to wear a funny hat?

DINAH. Not unless you want to. It's just that it could be a lot more dangerous than I led you to believe. You could really get lost.

MAGELLAN. I'm already lost.

DINAH. It's not funny. Time travel is like exploring the madness of God. It's like you're playing hide and seek with him. Only I keep getting him confused with my father. I think an unstable person might get themselves into a lot of trouble if they're not careful.

MAGELLAN. You think I'm unstable, just because I tried to kill my wife? You try spending five years with that woman.

You'd try to kill her, too.

DINAH. I don't know if unstable is the right word. I know you're very sad. Much sadder than you let on.

MAGELLAN. I'm not sad. I'm on top of the world.

DINAH. Your eyes are full of Magellanic clouds. You have a secret.

MAGELLAN. Everybody thinks they have secrets, but none of them really matters to anybody else.

DINAH. Yours does.

MAGELLAN. Come on. Teach me time travel.

DINAH. Well. Okay. I'll try. But if you get scared, just tell me you want to stop, and we'll stop, all right?

MAGELLAN. I can handle it.

DINAH. If you're going to do this, you've got to relax.

MAGELLAN. I'm relaxed.

DINAH. No you're not. You look relaxed, but you're not. You're very tense. Your shoulders are tense. Relax.

MAGELLAN. Okay.

DINAH. I don't know if this will work or not. I mean, I mostly do this by instinct. Maybe you're just not the sort of person who can do it.

MAGELLAN. Where are we going?

DINAH. We're not going anywhere. The easiest kind of time travel is to a different time at the same location, so we're just going to stay right here, only we're going back ninety or a hundred years or so, some time around the turn of the century. The grounds of this place used to be a park then. There was a carousel over there with horses and orchestrion music, you know, like the big music box barrel organ carnival type sound? There's this one afternoon I keep coming back to. It draws me for some reason.

MAGELLAN. Don't you have to know exactly when?

DINAH. Not really. It's like flipping through a zillion channels on the television set. You go very quickly, but you have this special sense of connection to certain particular moments in certain particular places. I don't know why.

MAGELLAN. But if you keep going back to the same place, don't you run into yourself?

DINAH. No. I think you must just automatically erase yourself when you go back to where you started. The only paradox in time travel is that there aren't any paradoxes. At least, not ones like that. Here. Hold my hand.

MAGELLAN. *(Taking her hand. They are sitting on the bench.)* Well, this is good.

DINAH. Calm down, sailor. This is just so you can stay with me. Now close your eyes and try to relax. It's like flipping back through the pages of a book. You see these flashing lights at first. Light and dark and light and dark and light and dark. It's days and months and years passing, only backwards. Keep your eyes closed until I tell you.

MAGELLAN. How can I see flashing lights if I've got my eyes closed?

DINAH. You see them in your head. Just shut up and pay attention. Here we go. Think about yesterday. Think about the day before yesterday. And the day before that. And the day before that. And the day before that. *(Lights begin to fade, and a flickering of dark and light begins, a strobe effect, like an old movie. It goes faster as she speaks.)* And the day before that. And the day before that. And the week before that. And the week before that. And the month before that. And the months before that. And the year before that. And the year before that. The year before that. And ten years before that. And ten years before that. Thirty years. And forty years. And fifty years. Seventy years. Ninety years. Okay, now we're slowing down. *(The flickering lights go more slowly.)* We're slowing down. We're almost there. We're looking for the carousel.

MAGELLAN. Where?

DINAH. Here. Right here in front of us. But don't open your eyes. Just listen. Listen for the carousel music. The carousel is playing music. The song is "The Band Played On." Do you know that?

MAGELLAN. Uh, no, I don't think. Wait. Casey is waltzing

a strawberry blond, that one?

DINAH. That's the one. I can hear it. Do you hear it? *(Very faintly, we can hear the carousel music, and the flickering of the lights is coming to a stop. The stage is lit rather dimly, and the light should give us an eerie sense that we have come to rest in another place.)* Do you hear it?

MAGELLAN. I can imagine it.

DINAH. But can you hear it?

MAGELLAN. In my imagination I can hear it.

DINAH. We're there now. We've come to a stop. Do you hear it? Tell the truth.

MAGELLAN. No.

DINAH. Listen with the inside of your brain.

MAGELLAN. Okay.

DINAH. Do you hear it now?

MAGELLAN. Maybe.

DINAH. Don't patronize me. Tell me the truth.

MAGELLAN. Okay. No. I don't. I don't hear it.

DINAH. Don't open your eyes until you hear it. I'm opening mine.

MAGELLAN. Okay. What do you see?

(Dim light. The music. As at the beginning, we see the YOUNG MAN sitting on the other bench, and the NURSE wheeling the baby carriage into view. They repeat exactly their actions we saw at the beginning.)

DINAH. There's a girl pushing a baby buggy. She's a nurse, I think. And there's a young man over there on another bench, he's very shy, you can tell. He's pretending to read, but actually he's been watching her. He comes here every day. He's been trying to work up the courage to talk to her.

MAGELLAN. How do you know this?

DINAH. I come here all the time, to this place in this moment. I love it here.

MAGELLAN. So is he ever going to talk to her?

DINAH. I don't know.

MAGELLAN. Why don't you just hop into the future and see?

DINAH. Because I don't like to do that. I like to savor the moments. When I find a place and a time I really like, I go back to the same place at the same time again and again, so I can really pay attention to it. Enjoy it. And maybe I'll arrive a minute or two earlier, or leave a minute or two later, now and then, so I'll gradually get a sense of what's happening around this moment, but it's a big mistake to be impatient about experience. You can see the whole universe in just one brief succession of moments in one place at one time, if you're just patient, and accept that moment, and savor it, don't try to rush past it.

MAGELLAN. Or, maybe you're just afraid to find out what happens.

DINAH. Maybe. Why shouldn't I be? Everything ends badly, doesn't it?

MAGELLAN. Can they see you?

DINAH. I think not when I first arrive. If I stay a while, I get more real to them. The longer you linger in a particular moment, the more danger there is you'll become so real that you get trapped there. I always leave when I start to feel like I'm becoming too real. I don't want them to notice me, I just like being here. Can you hear the music yet?

MAGELLAN. If I say yes can I open my eyes?

DINAH. Not unless you're telling the truth.

MAGELLAN. I'm opening them anyway. *(He opens his eyes. The past fades away with the music, the NURSE, the baby carriage, and the YOUNG MAN are gone.)* I don't see anything. Why don't I see anything?

DINAH. Because it's gone now.

MAGELLAN. So it's only there as long as I don't look at it?

DINAH. It's there whether you look at it or not. The point is to see it.

MAGELLAN. I was trying to see it. That's why I was look-ing at it. Only when I looked, it wasn't there. How come you can see it and I can't?

DINAH. I don't know. Maybe because your mind is messed up.

MAGELLAN. Your mind isn't messed up?

DINAH. Look, I don't know for sure, I'm just guessing here, but I think time is like a big, infinite series of interlock-ing movies or plays, and we're the characters in one set of movies while we're also the audience to some of the others—at least I am. You seem to be stuck in your own movie. Maybe because you feel guilty.

MAGELLAN. Guilty for what?

DINAH. You know what, don't you, Magellan? How much is she paying you?

MAGELLAN. I don't follow you.

DINAH. Oh, you follow me, all right. It's your job to fol-low me. How much is my sister paying you? Or is she just paying you off in sex?

MAGELLAN. I don't know what you mean.

DINAH. I saw her kissing you.

MAGELLAN. You're hallucinating.

DINAH. And you are a loathesome, scummy piece of float-ing sewage. Shame on you.

(DINAH starts to walk away.)

MAGELLAN. *(Grabbing her arm.)* Wait a minute.

DINAH. Let go of me.

MAGELLAN. I'm sorry.

DINAH. Let go of me or I'll call the guards.

MAGELLAN. I didn't come here to hurt you.

DINAH. Then let go of my arm.

MAGELLAN. She just wants your father's book. What's so wrong with that?

DINAH. You're sleeping with her, aren't you?

MAGELLAN. I don't see what that's got to do with anything. Yes. So what?

DINAH. So is she paying you, too?

MAGELLAN. I'm a private detective. It's my work.

DINAH. So she's paying you and also sleeping with you? Boy, she's even dumber than I thought she was.

MAGELLAN. She's not dumb. She's a very bright, very good person, and she loves you.

DINAH. I don't need you to defend my sister to me, okay?

MAGELLAN. She's worried about you.

DINAH. She wants the book.

MAGELLAN. Why won't you let her see it?

DINAH. Because she doesn't want to see it.

MAGELLAN. Of course she wants to see it.

DINAH. No she doesn't. She thinks she wants to see it, but she doesn't, trust me.

MAGELLAN. Why wouldn't she want to see it?

DINAH. It's none of your damned business. Go away.

MAGELLAN. My intention was not to hurt you in any way. Look, if you saw us kissing, and you knew I was sent here by your sister, then why did you go through all this stuff about teaching me to time travel?

DINAH. Because I liked you. Because I thought maybe if you could see what I see, if you could, I thought maybe you could—you might understand and then—oh, I don't know. It doesn't matter.

MAGELLAN. It does matter. Dinah, why wouldn't your sister want to see your father's book?

DINAH. Because it's about her.

MAGELLAN. It's about her?

DINAH. Hundreds of poems about her.

MAGELLAN. And you're jealous.

DINAH. No. Well, maybe, but, no. It isn't that.

MAGELLAN. Then what is it?

DINAH. Leave me alone.

MAGELLAN. Do you really hate her so much that you'd

put her through all this and yourself through all this just to spite her, just because you think your father loved her more than he loved you? Just because—

DINAH. They're poems about how a man can't stand it when other men look at his daughter's body. About how he hates it when they look at her. About how he hates her because he can't stop thinking about her. About how he loves his crazy daughter, but the other one, the beautiful one, he's obsessed with. I'm the crazy daughter he loves. She's the one he can't stop thinking about and wants to kill, because other men are always leering at her naked body, and she reminds him of his dead wife, and he can't stand it, and he thinks he's going crazy, and he can't tell anybody, and he can't explain it to anybody. There are poems about his fantasies of her being murdered. Of her naked murdered body lying on a bed. Poems about how he knew he had to kill himself or he'd kill her instead. Love poems. And hate poems. And mad poems. Our father killed himself. Did she tell you that? No, she didn't tell you that, because she doesn't believe it. But it's true. If you read the poems you know it's true. I can't let her see that book, all right? I just can't let her see it.

MAGELLAN. So you destroyed it?

DINAH. No. I couldn't destroy it.

MAGELLAN. Why not? If you're worried it would give your sister so much pain, why not just destroy it and be done with it?

DINAH. Because it was my father's. Because it was him. He wouldn't want that.

MAGELLAN. How do you know?

DINAH. Because if he'd wanted it destroyed, he'd have done it himself. Maybe he wanted her to see it, I don't know. Maybe it was his way of punishing her for—I don't know. I don't know.

MAGELLAN. So what did you do with it?

DINAH. I took it to the future.

MAGELLAN. You took it to the future?

DINAH. Yes. I took the manuscript a hundred years into the future and left it in the archives of a library where my father's other papers and things will end up, so somebody, some scholar or librarian will eventually find it and publish it.

MAGELLAN. But how could you—

DINAH. I did, that's all. I left it in the future. But you can't tell her, okay?

MAGELLAN. You think she'd believe that anyway?

DINAH. I mean the part about what's in it. You can tell her anything else you like, but not that. All right? Please? Magellan? She paid you to tell her where it is, not why I wouldn't give it to her. You can tell her it's in the future, that I've hidden it in the future, as long as you don't tell her why. Magellan? (Pause.) Do you love my sister?

MAGELLAN. I don't know.

DINAH. I think love is a kind of shared madness. Love is entering the abyss of another's soul, and sharing their madness. Don't you think that's true?

MAGELLAN. I don't know. I don't know anything.

DINAH. So you didn't really try to strangle your wife, huh?

MAGELLAN. I fantasized about it. Does that count?

DINAH. Kind of. (Pause.) Are you still married then?

MAGELLAN. No. My ex-wife is a photographer. She's the one that recommended me to your sister for this particular job.

DINAH. Well, that was big of her.

MAGELLAN. Not really. When I make money, she gets most of it anyway.

DINAH. I did so like your company. I mean, of all the lunatics here, you're the one I liked the best. Even though you're a really awful time traveller. (Pause.) You're going to tell her, aren't you?

MAGELLAN. The truth is, Dinah, I don't think you're connected very securely to reality. I don't know that I can trust what you say about the book or anything else.

DINAH. You think I'm crazy.

MAGELLAN. I think you've created a fantasy world out of your loneliness because reality disappoints you and hurts you and kills the people you love.

DINAH. And you haven't? *(Pause.)* Look, I'll make you a deal. If I can teach you to time travel, then you'll believe me, and you won't tell her about what's in the book, all right?

MAGELLAN. Dinah, we've already established that I can't do whatever it is that you do.

DINAH. But that was before.

MAGELLAN. Before what?

DINAH. Before I told you what's in the book. And while you were still lying to me about who you were. It was blocking you. The guilt, from lying. The betrayal. You don't like betrayal. You're not good at betrayal. The lying and the guilt were keeping you trapped in where you were. I bet you could do it now.

MAGELLAN. This is crazy, Dinah. You know it's—

DINAH. I felt something. When you were holding my hand, I felt something. I think you can do this. I think you're one of us. One of the people who can do this. One of the people they think are crazy, because we're different, and we can go to these places and see these things and hear this music and they can't. I could feel it. Just try. Just do this for me. Just once more. Please? If you care at all about me. What harm can it do? A little time travel. What have you got to lose? Where else have you got to go?

MAGELLAN. All right.

DINAH. Good. So, give me your hand. *(He gives her his hand, and they sit on the bench as before.)* Now, close your eyes. We're going back to that same place, that same moment as before, with the carousel music. Come on. Listen this time. Really listen. Think about yesterday. Think about the day before yesterday. And the day before that. And the day before that. And the day before that. *(Stage begins to flicker and darken, as before.)* And the day before that. And the day before that. And the week before that. And the week before that.

And the month before that. And the month before that. And the year before that. And the year before that. The year before that. And ten years before that. And ten years before that. Thirty years. And forty years. And fifty years. Seventy years. Ninety years. Now we're slowing down. *(The lights flicker more slowly, as before.)* We're slowing down. We're almost there. Listen for the carousel music, Don't open your eyes. Just listen. Can you hear it? *(Faintly, the sound of the carousel music.)* We've come to a stop. We're there. Listen. Can you feel it through my hand? Can you feel it? Don't open you eyes unless you can feel it. The other time. The other place. Listen. *(The YOUNG MAN is on the other bench, as before. And the NURSE appears with the baby carriage, all exactly as before.)* There's the pretty nurse with the baby carriage. And there's the young man over on the other bench. It's a late summer day. There's just the faintest hint of autumn in the air. The carousel music is playing. The young man is still trying to work up the courage to talk to her. The music is playing. In just a second she's going to drop the baby's stuffed animal on the ground. Wait. *(The NURSE drops the stuffed animal, as before.)* There it goes. The young man is looking at it. He wants to go and pick it up, but he's afraid. He's been hurt a lot. He's afraid that if he goes and talks to her, he'll break the spell, and she'll go away and never come back. But he wants to. And he knows that this is his moment. He can either take it, or lose it forever. Can you hear the music? Magellan?

MAGELLAN. I don't know.

DINAH. It's his moment. He's got to decide now. Time won't wait for him. He's not moving. He's just sitting there. Pick it up. Please pick it up. You love her. You know you love her. Oh, please pick it up. *(The YOUNG MAN gets up, goes over to the stuffed animal, and picks it up. He hands it to the NURSE.)* He did it. He picked it up. He's handing it to her. She's looking at him. They're talking to each other now. They're talking. Do you hear the music? Magellan, do you hear the music?

MAGELLAN. Maybe. I don't know. I think it's just my imagination.

DINAH. You hear it? You can hear it, can't you?

MAGELLAN. It isn't real.

DINAH. You hear it.

MAGELLAN. I don't think so.

DINAH. He's making her laugh. She likes him. She's blushing. Oh, this is good. This is so good. I wish you could open your eyes and see it. He's asking her to dance. She's saying no. Ask her again. Ask her again, stupid. Go on. This is your chance. This is your big chance. Don't screw it up. This could be your only chance in the entire history of the universe, and there is only this one moment, and when it's gone, it's always gone, forever. Ask her again. Do you hear the music? *(MAGELLAN doesn't answer.)* He's asking her again. She's going to dance with him. She's going to dance with him. If you can hear the music, open your eyes. Open you eyes and look. Magellan? Open you eyes and look. This could be your only chance. Magellan?

MAGELLAN. All right.

(The NURSE and the YOUNG MAN are dancing.)

DINAH. They're dancing. Oh, it's beautiful. Isn't it beautiful? *(MAGELLAN opens his eyes.)* What do you see, Magellan? Tell me what you see. You can hear the music, and you can see them dancing. You're here, Magellan. The asylum is gone. This is a much better place. This is the best asylum there is. This is the past. And it's forever. You can see it, can't you? You can hear the carousel music and you can see it, so you believe me, and you won't tell her now. You won't tell her, will you? You promised you wouldn't tell her if I brought you here. I'm so proud of that young man. He had his chance and he took it. You're right, I was always afraid to stay much longer, because I thought he probably wouldn't have the courage, that he'd let the moment go right by him, and then he'd

have lost her forever. But he didn't. He saw his moment and he took it, and now they're dancing. Isn't that how it should be? Don't you think?
    MAGELLAN. Yes.

(Pause.)

    DINAH. Magellan? Ask me to dance.

(Pause.)

    MAGELLAN. Would you like to dance?
    DINAH. Yes. Yes I would. Very much, thank you.

(DINAH stands, still holding MAGELLAN's hand. He stands, and gently puts his arms around her, and they dance. The two couples dance. Lights fade and go out. Just the carousel music in the darkness.)

END OF PLAY

THE
SIN-EATER

Sin-Eater: a person who in former times in certain parts of Wales, Scotland and England would through a ritual devouring of food and drink take upon himself the sins of the deceased. The food was often placed on the chest of the corpse. After the meal had been devoured, the sin-eater was driven from the house amid a hail of thrown objects and execrations.

CHARACTERS:

The Sin-Eater, a ragged young man
The Elder Sister, dressed in black
The Younger Sister, dressed in white

SETTING:

A room in a house in Wales in another time, and the shore by the mill race, downstage at the edge of the light. In the room is a bed and three wooden chairs.

THE SIN-EATER was first produced on December 9, 1996 at Actors Theatre of Louisville with the following cast:

Sin-Eater ....Tommy Schrider
Younger Sister ....Caitlin Miller
Elder Sister ....Missy Thomas

Directed by Simon Ha.
Dramaturg: Jenny Sandman

The play was later produced by Shadowbox Cabaret in Columbus, Ohio in the autumn of 1997 with the following cast:

Sin-Eater..Mark Slack
Younger Sister.....................................Carrie Lynn McDonald
Elder Sister...Julie Klein

Directed by Stacie Boord

THE SIN-EATER

*(Lights up on a bed and three wooden chairs on an otherwise
dark stage. A small house in Wales in another time. The
ELDER SISTER stands at the foot of the bed, in quiet mourn-
ing. The YOUNGER SISTER lies still in the bed. The SIN-
EATER, a poor young man, watches them.)*

THE SIN-EATER. My job always. Mother was before me.
Someone must do it, she said, and we have been chosen. It is
a dark privilege only we can acknowledge, she said. Their
contempt is our badge of honor. We are the closest, she said,
to understanding the mystery of Christ on earth. Like him, we
are the sin-eaters. Live in a shack at the edge of the village.
Shunned by all until their time of need. Someone dies, then I
am summoned. But this time it was a different thing. Oh, Jesus
help me. This time it was a different matter entirely. They
were two sisters, I had watched them since they were little
girls, the elder dark and quiet, the younger bright and lively,
and both so beautiful, their eyes and their hair, to see them
walk down green paths in spring, at water's edge in summer,
through red and gold woods in autumn, on ice in winter, oh,
those two, always together, always so lovely, the elder quiet,
watching, the younger laughing, teasing the boys. The elder
now and then took pity on me, brought me food, left it at the
gate for me, but the younger threw rocks and called me names
and laughed. I loved the younger. I loved the spirit of life in
her. It is true she ripped my heart out with her hands on all

43

occasions, and made jokes at my expense, but still I loved her, and could think no harm of her. Then came word I was wanted at their house. I hoped at first it was another cruel joke, but no. The younger had died suddenly. She lay dead now in her bed. I must come and do what only I could do. Oh, God, oh, God, this is a more exquisite punishment and torment than ever you have given me. To enter that house. I have dreamed of that house. In my dreams I have walked in that house, and come to that bed, and crept into it with my beloved. Now I must enter it and eat her sins from off her breast.

THE ELDER SISTER. Well, what are you gawking at? Come here, boy. What is wrong with you?

THE SIN-EATER. I'm sorry, I just—I'm sorry.

THE ELDER SISTER. You act as if you've never done this before.

THE SIN-EATER. I have done this many times.

THE ELDER SISTER. Then why do you hang back like a guilty dog? She is dead, boy. She can throw no more rocks at you now. Do you think to take your revenge upon her by refusing to eat her sins?

THE SIN-EATER. Revenge?

THE ELDER SISTER. I know that she was cruel to you, and did torment you. I am sorry for that. She meant no harm, I swear to you, she did not. She had such life in her, it must be bursting out in all directions. She had all the world in her. Every grief and joy, every love and hate—no, not hate, there was no hate in her, there was anger, and impatience, and perhaps now and then a cruel sense of humor, but she was gentle, and loving, and all animals loved her, and all souls on earth, but you, perhaps. You must not blame her for being young and sometimes thoughtless. She was a good girl, and meant no evil.

THE SIN-EATER. I never blamed your sister. She was welcome to throw rocks at me. I took great pleasure knowing that she lived. I grieve for her as you do.

THE ELDER SISTER. That is a very Christian thing.

THE SIN-EATER. No.

THE ELDER SISTER. Watch over her while I get the food.

THE SIN-EATER. Yes. I will watch over her. *(The ELDER SISTER looks at the corpse for a moment, then goes. He approaches the bed shyly.)* Oh, God. She is still ungodly beautiful. Even in death she seems to live. I cannot bear to think of her sweet body rotting in the earth. Jesus, Jesus.

(THE SIN-EATER falls to his knees and rests his forehead against the foot of the bed.)

THE YOUNGER SISTER. *(Lying motionless in bed.)* The problem is, I'm not dead. I mean, it would seem that I am dead, but the fact is, I can hear everything they say, I can hear the owls out my window, I can smell the flowers in my room, I have heard my sister sobbing over me, I felt her tenderly bathe my corpse, which was not at all an unpleasant sensation, except that I wanted to tell her I'm not dead, only I could not speak, I could not move, I could not even open my eyes, and yet my heart beats, slowly, slowly, but it beats, I want to scream at her that I am alive, but nothing comes out. It is some sort of epileptic fit, it must be, I remember our mother telling me once that our grandfather used to have these, that once he interrupted his own funeral by sitting up and announcing that he wanted some crackers. How can I let them know I'm alive? Perhaps I can pee. Let me try. Ooooo. Ooooo. Alas, nothing. Not a drop. If only I'd had that extra cup of tea before my unfortunate demise. Oh, dear. What if they bury me? What if they bury me? Hello. I'm in here. Please don't bury me. Oh, why can't they hear me? And what is that loathesome boy doing with his head at my feet? I wish he would keep away from my feet.

THE ELDER SISTER. *(Returning with a plate upon which are placed bread, cheese and wine.)* What are you doing?

THE SIN-EATER. Praying for her soul.

THE ELDER SISTER. It is not the job of the sin-eater to

pray. It is the job of the sin-eater to eat the sins of the dead, and thus take them upon himself. Here is the food. *(She puts the plate on the YOUNGER SISTER's chest.)* Are you ready? You don't look well, boy.

THE SIN-EATER. I don't know if I can do this.

THE ELDER SISTER. Of course you can do this. Why couldn't you do this? This is what you do. This is how you make your living, such as it is. If you don't eat my sister's sins from off her breast, who will? You are the only sin-eater in the village. What is it? Do you want more money?

THE SIN-EATER. No, no, it isn't the money. It's her.

THE ELDER SISTER. What's wrong with her?

THE SIN-EATER. Nothing. Nothing is wrong with her.

THE YOUNGER SISTER. I'm not dead, that's what's wrong with me.

THE ELDER SISTER. Then do your work and be done with it. There is bread and cheese and wine. Do you need anything else?

THE YOUNGER SISTER. I'd like some crackers.

THE SIN-EATER. No. This will be fine.

THE ELDER SISTER. I will be just in the next room. Let me know when you're done.

THE SIN-EATER. Yes. I will.

THE ELDER SISTER. I still can't believe she's dead.

THE YOUNGER SISTER. Me neither.

THE ELDER SISTER. She looks so lovely there.

THE SIN-EATER. Yes.

THE ELDER SISTER. Well. I'll go then. Don't take forever.

THE YOUNGER SISTER. Don't go. Don't leave me alone with this revolting person. I'm not dead. I'm not dead. Look, I'm attempting to pee.

(THE ELDER SISTER goes. THE SIN-EATER looks at the body.)

THE SIN-EATER. So sweet she looks. So innocent.

THE YOUNGER SISTER. I'm not dead, you simpleton. Can't you tell I'm breathing, you great, foul-smelling ignoramus?

THE SIN-EATER. I must eat her sins now. I must eat her sins. This is the one thing I can do for her. This is the only act of love which is permitted of me. I will never love another. I have only loved her. I will only love her. She is all the world to me. And now she lies here dead before me on her bed.

THE YOUNGER SISTER. I'm alive, you jackass. You blockhead. You lip-diddling imbecile. Can't you see that I'm alive? Get this crap off my chest and get away from me. You smell like a small animal has died in your pants.

THE SIN-EATER. I'm not hungry.

THE YOUNGER SISTER. Well, I am. I'm starving to death. Could I have a piece of that cheese if you don't want it?

THE SIN-EATER. I am so unhappy, I cannot eat.

THE YOUNGER SISTER. I can eat. I can eat. Just give me a drink of wine, why don't you? Listen to me, bean head. Hello? Hello? An important message for the village idiot. Your beloved is not yet ready for the maggot farm. Hello?

THE SIN-EATER. Oh, God. I am having evil thoughts. I am having evil thoughts.

THE YOUNGER SISTER. Uh oh. I don't like the sound of that.

THE SIN-EATER. I must resist these evil thoughts. But I have loved her for so long. And now, to be alone with her, here in her bedroom—

THE YOUNGER SISTER. Help. Somebody help. Necrophilia. Necrophilia.

THE SIN-EATER. I have dreamed so often of this moment. Except of course she was not dead. Sleeping, perhaps. Oh, I must kiss her. Just once, just once before they put her in the cold earth, I must kiss her perfect lips.

THE YOUNGER SISTER. He is not going to kiss me. He is not going to kiss me.

THE SIN-EATER. I am going to kiss her.

THE YOUNGER SISTER. He is going to kiss me. He is going to kiss me. Now I wish I really was dead. Oh, oh, this is disgusting. This is disgusting. This—*(THE SIN-EATER very tenderly and reverently puts his lips to hers and kisses her, a long, long, very sensual kiss. Then he pulls back.)* Jesus, James and Mary.

THE SIN-EATER. Oh, God.

THE YOUNGER SISTER. Oh, God.

THE SIN-EATER. This is a terrible thing, what I've done. This is a terrible, terrible thing.

THE YOUNGER SISTER. A terrible thing. Do it again.

THE SIN-EATER. And what's even worse, I'm going to do it again.

THE YOUNGER SISTER. Oh, good, he's going to do it again. He's going to do it again.

(THE SIN-EATER kisses her again, long, reverential, and very erotic. In the middle of this the ELDER SISTER returns, sees them.)

THE ELDER SISTER. Just what the devil do you think you're doing?

THE SIN-EATER. *(Jumping away from the body.)* Ahhhh. Oh, I was just, I was—it's part of the ritual, we—

THE ELDER SISTER. Get the hell away from my sister. You despicable, monstrous creature. Get away from her. Get out. Get out of here. Get out. *(She is pulling him away, beating and kicking him.)* Out. Get out. Vermin. Excrement.

THE SIN-EATER. But I love her. I love her.

THE ELDER SISTER. I will tell the men of the village, and they will tear you to pieces, you vicious, evil, filthy, filthy man. Get. Get out. Get out.

(THE ELDER SISTER chases THE SIN-EATER away. He moves downstage and sits on the ground at the edge of the

light, in despair.)

THE YOUNGER SISTER. *(Sitting up in bed.)* Oh, no, you mustn't be mean to him.

THE ELDER SISTER. Mean to him? I'll be mean to him if I please. Do you know what that son of a—*(She looks at the YOUNGER SISTER, sees her sitting up.)* AHHHHHHHHHHHHHHHHHHH.

THE YOUNGER SISTER. AHHHHHHH. Don't shriek at me like that. Do you want to kill me all over again?

THE ELDER SISTER. What is happening here? Am I going mad? Have you come back from the dead?

THE YOUNGER SISTER. I was sleeping. Don't you remember about Grandpa and the crackers? Which reminds me, God I'm hungry. What have we got to eat around here? *(Grabbing the plate with the SIN-EATER's food on it.)* Oh, this looks good.

(THE YOUNGER SISTER begins to eat.)

THE ELDER SISTER. I don't understand this. I don't understand this at all. We had already dug the hole in the back yard.

THE YOUNGER SISTER. Maybe we can plant some azaleas. Now, run and get me some more food. Hurry. And bring back the Sin-Eater.

THE ELDER SISTER. You don't want to see that wretched man. He tried to molest you while you were dead.

THE YOUNGER SISTER. *(Chomping on the bread.)* He kissed me. He brought me back to life. It was incredible. My toes are still tingling. Go and get him. I want to see him. Now. Or I might drop dead again.

THE ELDER SISTER. All right, all right.

(THE ELDER SISTER runs out.)

THE YOUNGER SISTER. *(Sitting on the bed and eating, yelling after her sister.)* DO WE HAVE ANY LAMB CHOPS?

THE SIN-EATER. I've kissed the dead lips of my beloved. Nothing else matters now. The men of the village will come and tear me to pieces. I don't mind. I would rather be dead with her. I think I will just lie down here in the water. Yes, I will just lie down here and remember her kiss and let the water creep up over my head.

(THE SIN-EATER lies down on the stage, as if lying back in water, and is still.)

THE YOUNGER SISTER. FOOD. I WANT MORE FOOD. AND WHAT THE HELL KIND OF CHEESE IS THIS? IT TASTES LIKE FUNGUS.

THE ELDER SISTER. *(Returning with a plate of food.)* This is all we have left in the house.

THE YOUNGER SISTER. Great. Where is my Sin-Eater? I want my Sin-Eater.

THE ELDER SISTER. Listen, dear. I have some bad news for you, but I hope it will not spoil your resurrection. The Sin-Eater has drowned himself in the mill race. They have laid his body out there on the shore.

THE YOUNGER SISTER. He's dead? The Sin-Eater is dead? Are you sure? Couldn't he be sleeping just as I was? Couldn't it be like Grandpa and the crackers? Maybe it's contagious.

THE ELDER SISTER. No, dear. I am sorry. He is drowned.

THE YOUNGER SISTER. Oh. Oh, no.

THE ELDER SISTER. Here. Have some more food.

THE YOUNGER SISTER. I have lost my appetite entirely. Why would he drown himself?

THE ELDER SISTER. It must have been guilt for kissing your corpse. He didn't know you only slept.

THE YOUNGER SISTER. Oh, poor boy. Poor lonely creature. He never knew. He never knew. He saved me and he never knew. And what about his sins? Who will eat his sins for him? There is no sin-eater to eat his sins. He has died with his sins upon him, and all the sins he has eaten, and there is no one to eat his sins. I must go to him.

THE ELDER SISTER. You're not strong enough. You've just got over being dead.

THE YOUNGER SISTER. I must go to him, now. He needs me.

THE ELDER SISTER. What could he need you for? The man is dead.

THE YOUNGER SISTER. I must eat his sins.

THE ELDER SISTER. You cannot eat his sins. You'll be shunned as he was. They will throw stones at you and spit at you.

THE YOUNGER SISTER. I don't care. I don't care. I must eat his sins. Someone must eat his sins. He gave me life and I must eat his sins. *(She takes the new plate of food and goes to the edge of the light, where the SIN-EATER lies still.)* Hello. I've brought you some food. Here. *(She carefully puts the plate of food on his chest.)* I'm going to eat your sins now. I think it's only right. I don't care if they shun me, if they throw rocks and jeer at me and spit at me. You kissed me. You gave me life. I want to do this thing. This is what love is, I think. The eating of the other's sins. And yet I have no appetite. You are really quite beautiful, you know. *(Pause. She looks at him.)* Perhaps just one kiss first. Would that be all right? You would not mind, I think. Just one kiss before I eat your sins.

(THE YOUNGER SISTER gets down on her knees, bends over him, and kisses him long and tenderly on the lips. The EL-DER SISTER watches. The light fades on them and goes out.)

END OF PLAY

BALLERINAS

Ballerinas

In the dressing room before the show
the ballerinas are smoking cigars
and telling dirty stories, eating
potato chips and farting. They
like to play practical jokes.
whoopee cushions are popular here.
The ballerinas chew tobacco and
goose each other, watch television,
drink from flasks and swallow
goldfish, quarrel, pinch and hurl
tapioca pudding at the mirror.
But when the overture begins
they are magically transformed,
the goddess of swans descends
and all is forgiven.

5/79

CHARACTERS

Petroushka
Scheherazade
Giselle

SETTING

The backstage dressing room of an old theatre.

BALLERINAS

(Sound of Swan Lake, *and lights up on the backstage dressing room of an old theatre. Three ballerinas, Petroushka, Scheherazade and Giselle, appear. They are delicate, graceful and exquisitely beautiful creatures.)*

PETROUSHKA. Christ, I need a drink.

SCHEHERAZADE. I want you to know I think it's extremely unprofessional to drink during a performance.

PETROUSHKA. But it's all right to smoke cigars?

SCHEHERAZADE. *(Lighting up a fat cigar.)* That's different.

PETROUSHKA. How is it different? You don't need your lungs to dance? *(She drinks from a flask and looks at GISELLE, who is cocking her head to one side in a decidedly odd fashion.)* Giselle, are you all right? *(To SCHEHERAZADE.)* Is she all right? She looks pale.

SCHEHERAZADE. She always looks pale. She's a dancer.

PETROUSHKA. I think I'm growing a mustache again. It just keeps coming back like crab grass.

SCHEHERAZADE. Why don't you let it alone?

PETROUSHKA. If I let it alone, I'll have to join a barbershop quartet. Watch out for that puddle over there. The ceiling is leaking again. Why does it always rain on performance nights? That stage is so warped, it's like dancing on a giant nose.

SCHEHERAZADE. I think a mustache can be very attractive on a woman. My problem is, I've got feet like vulture claws. They look like they belong on the bottoms of Victorian furniture legs. And I have no ass. I'd give anything to have an ass. All my life I've dreamed about having a real ass.

PETROUSHKA. Do you want part of mine?

SCHEHERAZADE. Now, you've got an ass. You've got two asses.

PETROUSHKA. No, I've got it down to an ass and a half. I've been working out.

SCHEHERAZADE. Dancing is working out.

PETROUSHKA. Dancing is work.

SCHEHERAZADE. Working out is work.

PETROUSHKA. Everything is work.

SCHEHERAZADE. Sex isn't work.

PETROUSHKA. Then I must be doing it wrong.

SCHEHERAZADE. Breathing is work.

PETROUSHKA. It wouldn't be if you'd stop smoking those damned cigars.

SCHEHERAZADE. I need to smoke. Smoking is my life.

PETROUSHKA. I thought dancing was your life.

SCHEHERAZADE. Dancing is something I do when I'm not smoking. If somebody would write a ballet I could dance while smoking a Cuban cigar, I'd die a happy woman.

PETROUSHKA. Do we have any Spam left?

SCHEHERAZADE. You ate it all yesterday. I think at least one entire buttock of one of your asses is almost entirely made up of Spam.

PETROUSHKA. Spam is not fattening. Spam is God's most perfect food. And I didn't eat it all. I think the rats must have gotten it. I saw a rat in here last week as big as Nijinsky.

SCHEHERAZADE. *(Watching Giselle tilt her head to the side and move her neck back and forth.)* Giselle, what the hell are you doing? What's the matter with you?

GISELLE. I don't want to be a swan anymore. I am weary of being a bird. I hate this. I really hate this. Being a bird sucks.

PETROUSHKA. You're not a bird, Giselle. You're just impersonating a bird for a living. Or you would be, if they were still paying us. Aren't they ever going to pay us again? The stage floor is rippled like a potato chip, the backstage is a swamp, the rats eat my Spam, and I haven't seen a pay check since I only had one ass.

GISELLE. And I've turned into a swan.

SCHEHERAZADE. You have not turned into a swan.

GISELLE. But I've been having these swan dreams. I'm in a pond. I'm a pond swan. And I'm swimming, and picking bugs out of my feathers, and peeing in the water.

PETROUSHKA. Swans don't pee in the water, do they?

SCHEHERAZADE. No, they pee in spittoons. Where did you think swans pee?

PETROUSHKA. I've never seen swans pee in cartoons.

SCHEHERAZADE. Not cartoons. Spittoons. Pay attention, Petroushka.

PETROUSHKA. I can't pay attention. I'm starving to death. Anyway, I don't think dreaming about peeing in the water means you're a swan, honey. People don't turn into swans. It's just a story, like when somebody tells you they love you. So, who really ate my Spam?

SCHEHERAZADE. I didn't eat your Spam.

GISELLE. But I've been growing feathers. It's true.

SCHEHERAZADE. You're not growing feathers.

GISELLE. There are feathers all over my apartment. I think I'm molting.

SCHEHERAZADE. It's from your feather boa.

GISELLE. I don't have a feather boa. I hate snakes. I'm a swan, and I'm molting, and I think this is the end of my dance.

PETROUSHKA. Let's go over and ask the boys if they took our Spam.

SCHEHERAZADE. Will you just shut up about the damned Spam? Why are you so fixated on Spam? Giselle is having a nervous breakdown and peeing in the water and all you can think about is canned pigs' tongues.

PETROUSHKA. She's not having a nervous breakdown.

SCHEHERAZADE. She's molting.

GISELLE. Last night I think I laid an egg.

SCHEHERAZADE. You didn't lay an egg.

PETROUSHKA. I wish I had some Spam and eggs. You know, in France, Spam is considered a great delicacy. They always eat it when they go to Jerry Lewis movies.

GISELLE. I woke up and there was an egg in my bed, and I couldn't sit down all morning. It was a very large egg.

PETROUSHKA. There must be some rational explanation for that.

SCHEHERAZADE. Like what?

PETROUSHKA. Well, maybe she's got an ostrich in her apartment. That would explain both the egg and the molting.

SCHEHERAZADE. She's got an ostrich in her apartment and she doesn't know it?

PETROUSHKA. Maybe it hides during the day and just comes out at night. They're known to be shy except while mating or when otherwise annoyed. And their feet look very much like yours.

GISELLE. Swans are ugly when they're young, and so was I. Swans mate for life. So do I.

SCHEHERAZADE. I didn't know you mated at all. Now, Petroushka, she mates.

PETROUSHKA. Only during mating season.

SCHEHERAZADE. When is it not mating season?

PETROUSHKA. When I'm eating.

SCHEHERAZADE. Who did you mate with, Giselle?

GISELLE. It all makes sense. Swans eat shellfish and seeds and roots and so do I.

PETROUSHKA. What I'd really like is a pound cake.

GISELLE. Swans eat worms and so do I.

SCHEHERAZADE. Giselle, you don't eat worms.

GISELLE. All my life I've been eating worms.

PETROUSHKA. I don't think I could eat worms. Maybe in a meat loaf. I'd kill for a nice, steaming meat loaf, with A-1 sauce all over it.

GISELLE. Men are worms, and all my life I've been eating them, and now I'm sick. I'm sick, Scheherazade. I'm a sick, sick swan.

SCHEHERAZADE. Giselle, would you like to go and lie down for a few minutes?

GISELLE. Some swans are mute, and I am mute.

SCHEHERAZADE. You're not mute.

GISELLE. Yes I am.

SCHEHERAZADE. No you're not.

GISELLE. Yes I am. I'm mute. I'M MUTE. I'M MUTE. I'M MUTE.

SCHEHERAZADE. You're not mute. You're talking now. If you're talking, then you're not mute. Think about it.

GISELLE. I'm not talking. Swans can't talk. Some swans whistle. Some swans trumpet. Perhaps some play the saxophone, I don't know, but not I. I do not whistle, or trumpet, or play any musical instruments whatsoever, because I am one of the mute swans. They have cut out my tongue, and I have only my body left to speak with, and the body is a frail instrument, and highly inadequate for most practical purposes. It is beautiful for a moment, but then it grows uglier and uglier. The body becomes a stranger, and then in the end it kills the swan, and the swan screams and screams, but nobody can hear, because the swan is mute.

PETROUSHKA. Boy, and I thought I was having a bad day. You need a drink.

GISELLE. I've eaten too many worms, and my body hurts. It hurts all the time. I am sick of the first position. I am sick of the second position. I am sick of the last position. I am sick of the missionary position. I am sick of all possible positions. And I need to journey now to the place where the mute swans go to scream.

PETROUSHKA. Well, you better do it fast, kid, because we've got to get back onstage in a minute.

GISELLE. I am a dead swan. The swan is dead.

SCHEHERAZADE. No, no, the swan isn't dead. The swan is just a little discouraged by life.

GISELLE. The swan is dead. The swan has choked to death on worms. The swan is not loved, except for her magnificently sleek body, and her breathtaking but transitory good looks. All positions now make this swan nauseous. This swan is a drooping bird. There is no more song in this mute birdy. She has done with art, and life, and princes, and peeing in the lake. There shall be no more swans in this place forever.

SCHEHERAZADE. But we've got to go back on now.

GISELLE. Not me. I'm a dead birdy. The dead birdy does not dance.

SCHEHERAZADE. Come on, sweetie. We can't go out there minus a swan. People will notice. It'll screw up the symmetry.

GISELLE. Nobody will notice, because shortly before swans die, they become invisible. I am an invisible dead swan.

SCHEHERAZADE. You're not invisible. I can see you.

GISELLE. Only because you're another swan. You're dying, too. All the swans are dying. Nobody loves us any more. The theatre is falling apart. The audience is made of corpses. We have peed too many times in the lake. Now we must bury all the dead swans.

(She sits on the floor and curls up into a ball.)

SCHEHERAZADE. Giselle. Giselle, get up. You're going to get us all fired. Giselle? Come on, kid. Get up. *(She tries to pull GISELLE to her feet. GISELLE is lifeless and floppy.)* Petroushka, give me a hand here, will you?

PETROUSHKA. Actually, I don't feel so good myself. And I've been noticing these mysterious feathers all around my apartment lately. Maybe I'm molting, too. Maybe we're all molting. And dying. We're all dying.

SCHEHERAZADE. You're not molting. You're drunk.

PETROUSHKA. Maybe I'm drunk because I'm dying.

Everything is dying. Our company is losing all its grants, one by one. This place will be a Chucky Cheese next year. Our endowment has been eaten by pigs. She's right. We're dying. All the swans are dying. Soon the world will be entirely inhabited by vultures, snakes and pigs. They will all eat money and fried excrement and each other, and there will be no more swans. All the swans will be dead and gone, and the only thing left will be a few feathers. In time, nobody will be able to imagine what a swan looked like. Swans will be a precious, fading memory in some crabby old dance teacher's head. All the swans are dying. This is the swans' burial ground.

(She curls up on the floor, cuddling GISELLE in her arms.)

SCHEHERAZADE. We are not dying. I am not dying. This is not the place where the mute swans go to scream. This is not the mute swans' burial ground. And I am not— *(She reaches into her cleavage, as if to scratch something under her breast, and pulls out a large feather.)* —molting. *(She stares at the feather.)*

We have always been. And we shall always be. Because all the universe is the dance of Shiva. And swans never die. They never die. They are simply transformed into beautiful princesses who live forever in fairy tales, and the tales go on forever, the telling goes on forever, and the dance goes on forever, there is no end to the telling of tales, and in these tales each night they dance, the telling of tales is the dance of the goddess. Pigs do not kill the dance. Pigs do not kill beauty. All is transformed. All is transformed forever. Swans are forever. For this is the nature of telling. And this is the nature of dance. And this is the nature of swans.

(SCHEHERAZADE looks at the feather. Sound of Swan Lake as lights fade on them and go out.)

END OF PLAY

THE LOST GIRL

When casting the runes
one must always remember
to twist one's body
into the shape of the rune
and yodel.

—Fragment from an Occult Notebook

CHARACTERS

Lara
Mala
Nola

SETTING;

A park bench in a foreign country.

THE LOST GIRL

(A park bench. LARA sits there, reading a book with a black cover. Birds sing. MALA enters from left, wearing a back pack, and holding a map. Both girls are in their early twenties, and both are dressed in bluejeans and tee shirts.)

MALA. Excuse me.

LARA. Futhorc?

MALA. Could you tell me how to get to Yggdrasil?

LARA. Meyognyfal. Nospisit zeno.

MALA. No, uh, Yggdrasil. Look, it's right here on the map, but I can't seem to fit the map to where I am. I mean, some of the places around here are on the map, but some of them aren't, and some of them are in different places than they're supposed to be. *(She begins unfolding the map. It is enormous and very awkward.)* Could you help show me where I am on the map?

LARA. Map?

MALA. Yes. Map. Where am I on the map?

LARA. *(Making the sign of the cross with her fingers in the direction of the map.)* Neyemon oxor. Demoni. Demoni.

MALA. No, it's just a map. Look. It's a map. You've seen maps. It's a map.

LARA. Map est demoni.

MALA. Well, maybe, but it's all I've got, because I'm lost.

LARA. Lost?

65

MALA. Yes. I'm lost. Can you help me?

LARA. Sorven die eboln.

MALA. Pardon? Wait, I've got my phrase book here somewhere. Sorven is—I don't know what sorven is. Eboln is—don't tell me—I know that one—

LARA. *(Lifting up MALA's arm and pointing at her elbow.)* Eboln. Vretty.

MALA. Oh. Elbows. Eboln is elbows.

LARA. Elbows. Vretty vretty elbows.

MALA. You like my elbows?

LARA. Elbows vretty vretty gemolkin.

MALA. Well, thank you. I think. So, your people find the elbows an attractive part of the body, do you?

LARA. Elbows. Gemolkin elbows traducant.

MALA. That's very interesting. You see, that's exactly the sort of cultural differences that I find so fascinating when I travel. I mean, in my country, people hardly ever take the trouble to stop and admire a person's elbows. But here, apparently, that's, uh, what you do.

LARA. Eboln nix demoni cum scarca ziss.

MALA. What? Elbows protect you from demons?

LARA. Scarca ziss. Pretskon yugal modrisan die eboln nix demoni. Skogs-snuf.

MALA. I see. Well, actually, I don't really see. I kind of see, but I don't exactly see, and I'm never quite sure if I really see or if I'm just kidding myself and in fact we're actually talking about wart hogs or something.

LARA. Wart hogs.

MALA. Wart hogs. Right.

LARA. *(Nodding her head thoughtfully.)* Wart hogs.

MALA. *(Taking off her back pack and sitting down on the bench with LARA.)* Don't worry about it. It's probably not an expression that's going to come up in everyday conversation very much. The thing is, I've been running across a lot of words that aren't in my phrase book. It's very discouraging when the map is wrong and the phrases aren't in the phrase book, or the phrase book is wrong because it's out of date or was written for a slightly different region of wherever the hell it is I am, and people seem to be telling you there's demons in your elbows and you're not sure what exactly they're trying to get at, but you figure it must be important except you can't imagine how it could be, but you're not sure. You're never really sure, when you're in a foreign country. And I want to tell you, and no offense meant, but this is a pretty weird country you've got here.

LARA. Weird.

MALA. Yes. Intensely weird. And yet kind of familiar. I mean, sometimes it almost looks like home, but then some things are so different here, like, for one thing, there's mirrors everywhere.

LARA. Mirrors?

MALA. Yes. Mirrors. Here. *(She takes out a compact from her back pack and opens it. Points.)* Mirror.

LARA. *(Looks in the mirror, then at MALA, then back in the mirror.)* Mirror?

MALA. Yes. This country is full of mirrors. I've never seen so many mirrors. There's mirrors all over the place. Half the time you don't know if you're looking at the real thing or just a reflection, or a reflection of a reflection. Do you know what I mean?

LARA. Reflection.

MALA. Right. And yet, it's a weird thing, but at the same time I've been having this uncanny feeling that I've been here before. Or that—I don't know. It's like I keep almost remembering things. Sometimes I have no idea what the people here are saying, but other times I think I know what the words mean better if I don't try to look them up. Do you understand? It's as if I only know it if I don't try to get to it through somebody else's version of what it's supposed to mean. Does that make any sense to you? There are some words that I just seem somehow to almost know what they stand for. Like, um, noskoy.

LARA. Noskoy.

MALA. It means darkness, right?

LARA. Darkness. Noskoy.

MALA. Exactly. And mornas is like clocks or—

LARA. Clockworks.

MALA. Oh, you know that word? Good. Very good. This place is full of clocks, too. Mirrors and clocks. It's like the whole country is one big festival of ticking and chiming and cuckoos.

LARA. Mornas. Clockworks. Noskoy. Darkness. Sonnendalg.

MALA. Sundial.

LARA. Sundial.

MALA. See? Was I right? Sonnendalg is sundial. I was just guessing, I swear, but I was right. This place is also full of sundials. Except a lot of them are in the shade, which is also, I guess, a cultural difference, because where I come from, we usually put our sundials in the sun. That is, I think we would if we had sundials, which mostly we don't. Do you know what it's like? It's almost like I used to live here, a long, long time ago. Borten norcas.

LARA. A long time ago.

MALA. Yes. And another thing. The windmills.

LARA. Caliban.

MALA. Yes. They're everywhere. Caliban is windmills?

LARA. Caliban. Windmills. *(Running her hand along the back pack and admiring it.)* Gap.

MALA. Gap? Oh, yes. You like it?

LARA. Vretty.

MALA. Yes. It is really nice, isn't it? My mother gave me that, when I started out on my travels. I've been gone so long, it's like everything I own is in there now. Everything else, everything from before, is like a dream. Do you know what I mean?

LARA. *(Touching the back pack.)* Nice.

MALA. Do you want to try it? Go ahead. It goes on like this. See? *(She helps LARA put the back pack on.)* There. It looks good on you.

LARA. Nice. Gap.

MALA. Absolutely. Do you travel? Have you travelled?

LARA. Like a dream. A long time ago.

MALA. Yes, but do you ever get the urge to travel?

LARA. I've been gone so long.

MALA. I know what you mean. I know exactly what you mean. And yet this place, you know, it has, I mean, it has its own kind of strange beauty, this place.

LARA. Strange.

MALA. Yes. I mean, the sonnendalg, and the calibans, and the mirrors. What's the word for mirrors?

LARA. Mirrors.

MALA. Miranska-glas.

LARA. Yes. Everything I own is in there now.

MALA. Yes. It is. Well, you know, I think it's time to go now.

LARA. Time to go.

MALA. Off to find Yggdrasil.

LARA. Off to find Yggdrasil.

MALA. *(Picks up the map.)* I guess it's better to just put away the map and trust your instincts, huh? Map. Demoni.

LARA. *(Taking the map from her hand and looking at it.)* Map.

MALA. Demoni. *(Pause.)* So. I'll be saying good-bye now.

LARA. Good-bye.

MALA. Good-bye.

(LARA gets up, shakes MALA's hand, and goes off right, wearing the back pack and holding the map. MALA sits there. Sound of the birds. She picks up LARA's black book, opens it, looks at it, turns it upside down and begins to read. NOLA enters from left, a girl in her early twenties, wearing bluejeans and a tee shirt, wearing a back pack and carrying a map.)

NOLA. Excuse me.

MALA. Futhorc?

NOLA. Could you tell me how to get to Yggdrasil?

MALA. Meyogynfal. Nospisit zeno.

NOLA. Yggdrasil. Look. It's right here on the map, but I can't seem to fit the map to where I am. I mean, some of the places around here are on the map, but some of them aren't, and some of them are in different places than they're supposed to be. *(She begins unfolding the map. It is enormous and very awkward.)* Could you help show me where I am on the map?

MALA. Map?

NOLA. Yes. Map. Where am I on the map?

MALA. *(Making the sign of the cross with her fingers in the direction of the map.)* Neyemon oxor. Demoni. Demoni.

NOLA. No. It's just a map. Look. It's a map. You've seen maps. It's a map.

MALA. Map est demoni.

NOLA. Well, maybe, but it's all I've got, because I'm lost.

MALA. Lost?

NOLA. Yes. I'm lost. Can you help me?

(MALA looks at her as if she is trying to remember something. Sound of birds as the light fades on them and goes out.)

END OF PLAY.

THE BABEL
OF
CIRCULAR
LABYRINTHS

CHARACTERS

Borges, an old writer
Beatriz, a beautiful young woman

SETTING:

A vast library late at night. A table, a chair, a green
shaded lamp which makes a circle of light,
and darkness all around.

THE BABEL OF
CIRCULAR LABYRINTHS

*(It is night in the great library. BORGES, an old, blind writer,
sits at a table in a circle of light from a green shaded reading lamp, an old book open before him.)*

BORGES.
Why does a blind man not sit in the dark?
And why does he turn the pages
of an open book before him? And
why is a raven like a writing desk?
Everything in the labyrinth
is a riddle, of course. The labyrinth
is constructed of riddles as a chimney
is constructed of bricks.
The blind man leaves the reading lamp on
because he loves the feel of its warmth
on his face, in the cool of the library
darkness which surrounds him.
He turns the pages of the open copy
of an English translation of *Don Quixote*
on the table before him because
he loves the feel of the paper under
his fingers, and the smell of old trees
and dead epoxy horses, a dark tribute
to the great Rocinante. As for the raven
and the writing desk—

(Pause. He listens.)
I have heard a footstep somewhere.
Someone has entered the labyrinth.
Here in the Library of Babel,
in the Mirror of Enigmas,
in the midst of the Circular Ruins,
in the Garden of Forking Paths,
somebody is lurking in the darkness.
(Pause.)
I smell perfume. This can only be
construed as a promising development,
I think. Come out of the shadows,
my dear. I can tell by your scent
that you are very beautiful. And if
I am mistaken in this matter, I request
that you please refrain from disillusioning me,
since what we love is always, after all,
a work of art that we have fashioned
in our head, and the purpose of art
is not to reproduce what can be seen.
The purpose of art is to make things visible.
Paul Klee said that, and I
have enjoyed very much not seeing
his paintings for many years.
Do you speak, child? Please step
into the light so I can smell you better.
The heat from the lamp will create
an alchemical reaction with
your perfume and your perspiration
and I shall, with any luck,
become entirely intoxicated.
(A moment. Then BEATRIZ steps into the light. She is a beau-
    tiful young woman dressed in the fashion of 1929.)
That's better. Won't you tell me
who you are?

BEATRIZ.
Don't you know me?
BORGES.
I am blind.
BEATRIZ.
Does that mean you can't know me?
BORGES.
It means I have given up archery.
But you do sound quite familiar,
and you smell like someone
I used to dream about.
BEATRIZ.
You don't dream about me any more?
BORGES.
You smell like Beatriz Viterbo. Or rather,
a woman I once called Beatriz in a story.
But you certainly can't be her.
BEATRIZ.
I can't? Why can't I? Why am I not
permitted to be who I am?
BORGES.
Because she is dead.
BEATRIZ.
But how can a character
in a story be dead?
BORGES.
The woman I loved is dead.
The woman in the story is
somebody else.
BEATRIZ.
Any woman you love
is always somebody else.
Nobody you love
is ever who you love.
The beloved is always
a fabrication of the lover.

You have just admitted as much.
If I am not the woman
you loved whose name
was not Beatriz, or
the woman in the story
who was not the woman
you loved, then I am
the woman they both saw
when they looked in the
mirror, or the woman
you imagined they saw in the
mirror, and I have come
to you from deep within
the labyrinth of mirrors
to give you a gift.

(She places a knife on the table before him.)

   BORGES.
(Not touching it.)
You have put a knife on the table.
   BEATRIZ.
How can a blind man
see a knife on a table?
   BORGES.
Why is a raven like a writing desk?
   BEATRIZ.
Because both are stained
all over with blackness.

(Pause.)

   BORGES.
So it is you.
I have mourned for you
all my life, you know.

And I have seen you.
    BEATRIZ.
Where have you seen me?
    BORGES.
In the cellar, under the dining room,
if one lies on one's back and looks upwards
and focuses upon the nineteenth step,
one can see that point from which
all other points are visible,
a sphere whose center is everywhere
and whose circumference is nowhere.
I have seen you there, in the garden,
in your bath, in your bed.
It is much easier to be in love
with a woman who is dead.
Why have you come here
and put a knife on the table
before a blind man in a
library at midnight?
    BEATRIZ.
Look at me, and you will see.
    BORGES.
How can a blind man
look at a dead woman?
    BEATRIZ.
How can a blind man
not look at a dead woman?
    BORGES.
By opening his eyes.
Why is a raven
like a writing desk?
    BEATRIZ.
Because one sits on a dead man,
and the other a dead man sits at.

(Pause.)

BORGES.
You are death, come to me
in the guise of a beautiful
woman I cannot see.
    BEATRIZ.
I was never much for symbols
myself. I always preferred
shopping. But I have learned
in the Kingdom of the Dead
that one has little choice
in the matter of whether or not
one will be a symbol for
somebody else. If I am a symbol
of something or other for you,
that's your problem, not mine.
    BORGES.
Then what am I supposed
to do with this knife?
    BEATRIZ.
What do you want
to do with it?
    BORGES.
I want to pick it up.
    BEATRIZ.
Then pick it up.
    BORGES.
If I pick it up, I will die.
    BEATRIZ.
And if you don't pick it up,
you will not?
    BORGES.
If I don't pick it up
I won't know
what would have happened
if I had picked it up.
It is like the Garden

of Forking Paths.
If you take one path
you have lost the other paths
forever.
    BEATRIZ.
Unless of course you stumble
upon them again
at a later time.
    BORGES.
The same path
stumbled upon again
at a later time
is never the same path.
    BEATRIZ.
Then don't pick up the knife.
    BORGES.
You know I will pick up the knife.
    BEATRIZ.
How do I know that?
    BORGES.
Because I know it.
    BEATRIZ.
I don't care if you know it.
It is my nature not to care,
whereas you are a writer,
it is your nature to care
but to do nothing about it.
    BORGES.
What did you care for, Beatriz?
You must have cared for something
once, I mean besides shopping.
    BEATRIZ.
Why is a raven like a writing desk?
    BORGES.
Because neither one is you.
(Sound of the ticking clock. He reaches out one hand towards

the knife, not yet touching it, hesitates, then pulls his hand
back.)
And because both are you, as,
although your circumference is nowhere,
your center is everywhere.
        BEATRIZ.
I am neither a raven nor a writing desk.
I am the person who waits
at the center of your particular
labyrinth. Why do you not
touch the knife? Are you so afraid
of death? What do you think
death is, that you should be so
terrified of it?
        BORGES.
In my particular theology
when writers die
they become their books.
        BEATRIZ.
And what happens when
a beautiful woman dies?
        BORGES.
They become books, too.
        BEATRIZ.
So you think everything
turns into books?
        BORGES.
Only what can be written.
        BEATRIZ.
What happens to the rest?
        BORGES.
It becomes photographs, sonatas,
paintings, buildings, and dirt.
        BEATRIZ.
Then pick up the knife
and turn into a book.

BORGES.
When I am a dead man, what
will I see when I look in the mirror?
        BEATRIZ.
They will turn the mirrors to the walls
so you can't see anything.
        BORGES.
But what would I see if I could look
in the mirrors that will be turned
to the wall when I am dead?
        BEATRIZ.
Oh, who really cares?
Just pick up the knife.
        BORGES.
But in order to pick up the knife,
I must move my hand half way to the
table. And in order to move my hand
half way to the table, I must move
my hand half way to half way.
And in order to move my hand
half way to half way, I must move
it first half way to that point.
And since in order to reach any point
between where my hand is now, and
where the knife is on the table,
I must first reach a point half way
to that point, and half way to the point
that is half way to that point,
it seems clear to me that,
as much as I would like to,
I will never be able
to pick up that knife.
        BEATRIZ.
What?
        BORGES.
It's Zeno's paradox.

BEATRIZ.
Whose ducks? What about ducks?
What do I care about a pair of ducks?
Of course you can see no pair of ducks.
You can't see you own nose
in front of your face. You're as blind
as a bulldog doorstop.
    BORGES.
No. Zeno. The ancient Greek philosopher.
    BEATRIZ.
He raised ducks?
    BORGES.
Actually, he is better known
for his tortoise.
    BEATRIZ.
Why are we discussing old Greek men
who keep ducks and turtles?
Pick up the knife.
    BORGES.
Why do you want me to pick up the knife?
    BEATRIZ.
I don't know.
    BORGES.
Do you want me to die?
    BEATRIZ.
I don't like blind people.
    BORGES.
Why not?
    BEATRIZ.
Because they can't see me.
I like to be seen. I am at my best
when I am seen. When a person
I am talking to can't see me,
it puts me at an unfair disadvantage.
I might as well be ugly. This cannot
be a good situation.

BORGES.

So you want to kill me because I am blind?

BEATRIZ.

I want to kill you so you can see me.

BORGES.

Do you mean that when I am dead
I will have my vision back?

BEATRIZ.

It could happen.

BORGES.

But what if it doesn't? What if I die
and enter eternal darkness?

BEATRIZ.

I don't know. I don't know the rules.
All I know is that I was told
to bring you this knife.

BORGES.

Who told you?

BEATRIZ.

I don't know.

BORGES.

Did somebody hand it to you?

BEATRIZ.

I don't think so.

BORGES.

What were you doing before you came here?

BEATRIZ.

I must have been taking a bath.
I always take a bath
before I go out.

BORGES.

And before that?

BEATRIZ.

I don't know. I was sleeping, I think.

BORGES.

And before that?

BEATRIZ.
Before that, and before that, and
before that, my God, you men,
with your questions, and your
questions, and your questions.
What were you doing before
you were born? I don't care.
I don't care. Leave me alone.
    BORGES.
Forgive me. I only wished—
    BEATRIZ.
I was looking in the mirror.
    BORGES.
When?
    BEATRIZ.
I've just remembered. It just
popped into my head when I
was yelling at you. I was looking
in the mirror.
    BORGES.
And what did you see?
    BEATRIZ.
I saw myself looking in a mirror.
And in that mirror
I was looking at myself
in a mirror in which
I was looking at myself.
    BORGES.
And then?
    BEATRIZ.
And then I found myself here,
in this library, which is, I assure you,
not the sort of place I am likely
to find myself lurking about in,
and I had this knife, and it was
as if someone was whispering

in my ear, to put the knife
on the table before the blind man.
    BORGES.
Do you know whose voice it was
who was whispering at you?
    BEATRIZ.
Yes. I do.
It was your voice.

(Pause.)

    BORGES.
Ah. I see.
    BEATRIZ.
You don't see. You're blind.
How can you see? You mean
you understand?
    BORGES.
No. But I see.
It is something
I have always
expected.
    BEATRIZ.
What? What are you talking about?
Why did you whisper in my ear
to come here and put a knife
on the table before you?
    BORGES.
It wasn't me. It was Borges.
    BEATRIZ.
Borges?
    BORGES.
Yes.
    BEATRIZ.
But you're Borges.

BORGES.
Yes.
　　BEATRIZ.
Then it was you.
　　BORGES.
No. It was him.
　　BEATRIZ.
Who?
　　BORGES.
Borges.
　　BEATRIZ.
Why don't I just
take the damned knife
and kill myself with it?
　　BORGES.
Because that is not what he wrote.
　　BEATRIZ.
What who wrote?
　　BORGES.
Borges.
　　BEATRIZ.
The Borges who is not you.
　　BORGES.
Exactly.
　　BEATRIZ.
I am trapped here in a dark library
which is like a labyrinth
with a madman whom
I have just supplied
with a sharp knife,
and you are telling me
that there is another Borges
who is not you but
who has your voice
who has whispered in my ear
and made me come here?

BORGES.
He has written you. He has
written a story. This is
what he's written. He's finally
written the story
of my death.
BEATRIZ.
And is it my death as well?
Have you read that far in
the story? But you can't read.
You're blind. Unless it is
written in Braille, of course.
Have you read my death
with your fingertips?
BORGES.
If it is my death, then
it is also your death.
BEATRIZ.
That doesn't seem right.
Why is that?
BORGES.
Because when I die, you die as well.
BEATRIZ.
Is that really necessary?
BORGES.
I'm afraid it's unavoidable.
BEATRIZ.
Because he wrote it in the story?
BORGES.
Because he wrote it in the story, yes.
BEATRIZ.
Why don't we just kill him instead?
BORGES.
Because he lives in my head.
BEATRIZ.
He lives in your head?

BORGES.

Yes.

BEATRIZ.

The Borges who is not you?

BORGES.

Yes.

BEATRIZ.

And he's told you to kill me?

BORGES.

He has written a story which is us.
In the story you bring me the knife
and I pick it up. When I pick up the knife
I die. And when I die, you die as well,
since you're only alive in my head.

BEATRIZ.

I'm living in your head, too?

BORGES.

Yes, you are.

BEATRIZ.

Isn't it getting a little crowded
there in your head?
Can't one of us perhaps
escape through your nose
or something?

BORGES.

I'm sorry. There is no escape
from this particular labyrinth.

BEATRIZ.

How do you know?

BORGES.

Because I made it.

BEATRIZ.

You have a labyrinth in your head as well?

BORGES.

Yes.

BEATRIZ.

It's a great wonder your head has not
exploded a long time ago.

BORGES.

Yes, I often
marvel at that
myself.

BEATRIZ.

What if I pick up the knife
and throw it away?

BORGES.

You can't.

BEATRIZ.

Why can't I?

BORGES.

Try it and see.

BEATRIZ.

All right.

(Pause.)

I can't.

BORGES.

I know.

BEATRIZ.

Why can't I do this?

BORGES.

I am going to pick up the knife now.

BEATRIZ.

Yes.

BORGES.

Would you do something for me first?

BEATRIZ.

What?

BORGES.

Would you kiss me?

BEATRIZ.

No.

BORGES.
All right.

(Pause.)

BEATRIZ.
Well, perhaps.
(Pause.)
No, I don't think so. Sorry.
    BORGES.
It's all right. It isn't me anyway.
I have no face. I look in the mirror
and I see nothing.
    BEATRIZ.
Because you're blind.
    BORGES.
No. That's not the reason.
(Pause.)
Why is a raven like a writing desk?
    BEATRIZ.
Because I love you.
    BORGES.
Because a dead man
who is now a book
has written that it is.
(Pause.)
You love me?
    BEATRIZ.
Did I say that?
    BORGES.
I think you did.
    BEATRIZ.
It wasn't me. It was her.
    BORGES.
Who?

BEATRIZ.
Beatriz. The woman in your head.
    BORGES.
Then if the person I am not
is loved by the person you are not,
I am resigned to my fate.
I will pick up the knife.
    BEATRIZ.
All right.
*(A moment. Sound of a clock ticking. He reaches out his hand
    to just above the knife.)*
Good-bye.
    BORGES.
Because there is no time
all good-byes are an illusion,
there are no good-byes,
only stories.

(He picks up the knife.)

    BEATRIZ.
What do you see?

*(He looks at her. The light fades and goes out. Darkness, and
    just the ticking of the clock.)*

END OF PLAY

SEANCE

CHARACTERS

Florence Cook, a young medium
Sir William Crookes, a respected physicist
Katie King, an apparition

SETTING

A darkened room with one light over a green baize table
with three wooden chairs, and a wooden cabinet
just visible upstage. The year is 1875.

SEANCE

*(A darkened room. One light over a green baize table. FLO-
RENCE COOK, a pretty young woman, sits drinking. Be-
hind her we can just make out a large wooden cabinet.
Sound of a clock ticking somewhere.)*

FLORENCE.
Apparition. Spectral manifestation of.
Cabinet and ectoplasm. Spook flubdubbery, done with mirrors. Everything is
mirrors reflecting mirrors. The lost girl
is sucked into the looking glass. She has
been devoured at midnight by the
carousel horses in the house of mirrors.
Only some bones and bits of yanked out hair
remain of what was once
the Princess of Regret.
Where are you, spirit? I am summoning
you. Katie, you shameless little slut,
wheel out your spook and tit show, love.
Give us a kiss and show us your knickers.
*(She drinks. From the darkness, the sound of a door creaking
open.)*
Ah. What's this? What's this? An ectoplasmic
manifestation? Spooks? Spooks?
(Sound of footsteps approaching in the darkness.)
Something wicked this way stumbles. It is Death,

arriving to pick up his filthy laundry.

(SIR WILLIAM CROOKES steps into the light, a distinguished
    looking gentleman of middle age.)

CROOKES.
Florence?
    FLORENCE.
Why, no, I'm sorry to report, it isn't Death,
it's merely the apparition of the great
Sir Willy. What's the matter, Willy? Did you
think for just a moment I was her? Did you
hope for just an instant she'd popped out
like a Jack-in-the-box to snuggle up against
your manly chest?
    CROOKES.
Florence. You're drinking.
    FLORENCE.
Yes, but I do it very badly.
    CROOKES.
You know you mustn't drink.
    FLORENCE.
I prefer to think of it as
communicating with the spirit world
in a liquid form. Give us a kiss
and show us your knickers, Willy.
    CROOKES.
Florence, get hold of yourself.
    FLORENCE.
I try to refrain from holding myself
in mixed company. I much prefer
holding myself in the bath, although
now and then I have held myself
under the table. You should try it.
It might loosen you up a little, Bill.

CROOKES.
Florence, my god, what's come over you?
You're thoroughly intoxicated.
This is appalling.
    FLORENCE.
Then please just go away and be appalled
somewhere else for a while, could you?
Your mustache is making me nauseous.
    CROOKES.
My mustache?
    FLORENCE.
Yes. It's crawling all over your face
like a crazed tarantula.
Get it away from me. Go
to Mexico and release it in the desert.
    CROOKES.
I can't go away and leave you like this.
    FLORENCE.
I don't see why not. Everybody else has.
Of all the grotesque and ridiculous
characters ever to step upon the stage
of this baroque and tedious goat and monkey show
which is what passes for my life, only you
have had the unbelievably bad manners
not to cut and run at the earliest opportunity,
and frankly, Willy, I am here to tell you,
this spaniel devotion of yours is
beginning to get on my nerves.
    CROOKES.
I can't bear to see you this way.
    FLORENCE.
Then go somewhere and look at someone else.
Why must you stay and just keep gawking at me?
It makes me feel as if I were the dead squid
in the bottle at the carnival of fools.
Just go away. Why can't you go away?

CROOKES.

Because I care for you.

FLORENCE.

You don't care for me.

CROOKES.

Of course I do. You know I do.

FLORENCE.

You don't. You can't. You're speaking gibberish
at me. What would your precious Ellen say
if she could hear you blathering out your great
supposed affection for me?

CROOKES.

My wife would understand. Does understand.
She knows the time I spend with you is
absolutely central to my scientific work.

FLORENCE.

Your scientific work.

CROOKES.

Yes. My investigations into truth.

FLORENCE.

Investigations into truth.

CROOKES.

Yes.

FLORENCE.

I am, to you, in other words, a kind
of laboratory rat.

CROOKES.

Of course not.

FLORENCE.

But this is science, Willy. We are not
permitted to grow attached to our experiments.
Do you become this passionate about
your other laboratory animals?

CROOKES.

You're not a laboratory animal,
you are a lovely, gifted, and unique young woman,

and I am not at all ashamed to say
that I have come to care for you. Why is that
so difficult for you to comprehend?
    FLORENCE.
You were not supposed to care for me.
You were supposed to expose me.
Which in your dreams, at least, I know you have.
Stripped me entirely naked, as it were,
and investigated every part of me,
much of it with your tongue.
I think science has never been so thorough.
    CROOKES.
I've done nothing of the kind.
    FLORENCE.
You were in a trance at the time.
Don't you remember?
The sex organs always work better
when one is in a trance.
    CROOKES.
Florence, why must you be so vulgar?
    FLORENCE.
Because I am vulgar. I was born vulgar.
Father was vulgar. Mother was vulgar.
We were brought up vulgar. We took
communion at the East Vulgarian Church.
We spread Vulgarian jam upon our muffins,
and played accordions. Vulgarity
is my proud heritage as an Englishwoman.
    CROOKES.
You are not vulgar. You put on
this mask of vulgarity to hurt me.
    FLORENCE.
Oh, God forbid that little Florry Cook,
an insignificant butcher's girl from Hackney,
should ever hurt a celebrated man
of science like yourself, the dean of modern

physics, inventor of the Crookes tube
and idol of idiot worshippers,
the gallant aristocrat
who came to lift my petticoats
above my head and thereby to expose
my private parts unto the civilized world
and also to America.
    CROOKES.
I came here as a man of science, yes,
in good faith, to investigate your work,
in a spirit of perfectly dispassionate enquiry,
and in the course of my investigations
discovered two extraordinary things.
One, that I believe in you,
and two, that I care for you.
That I care deeply for you.
That in fact I love you.
I mean of course I love you
as a father loves his daughter.
    FLORENCE.
Oh, so now it's incest, is it? You
dare to speak to me of love? You dare
to sully my mock-virgin ears with that
most hideous of words? You call me vulgar,
you who have sunk to uttering the most
obscene of all words in the English language,
the sort of word a man like Tennyson
would use? Well, I am shocked. Willy, you don't
believe in me, you've just been rendered blind
and stupid by your lust.
    CROOKES.
My lust? You call it lust?
    FLORENCE.
Oh, call it what you like, I do not choose
to quibble over nomenclature with
an idiot while time is eating me

in little sawtooth ticks and chimes and burps
and my knickers have begun to chafe my thighs,
especially since it isn't even me
you think you love. It's her.
    CROOKES.
Her?
    FLORENCE.
Willy, it is a monumental waste
of time to feign stupidity when you
are so accomplished at the thing itself.
Remember Ockam's Razor.
And when you get a chance, why don't you go
and cut your throat with it, to save us both
the trouble of continuing this jabber.
You know well who I mean. You don't love me,
you pompous, blithering clotpole on a stick.
Can you not see? Your true love is a dead
imaginary girl named Katie King.
    CROOKES.
Katie King is a spiritual manifestation,
a personage you conjure up from the beyond
in your séances. It is you I care for.
    FLORENCE.
You stupid man. You stupid, stupid man.
You're so profoundly imbecilic that
you cannot even begin to comprehend
the magnitude of your stupidity.
For those who are merely ignorant there is
at least some hope that they might learn something
some day. But for an educated moron
like yourself, there is no hope, since he's already
convinced that he knows everything.
    CROOKES.
I know I care for you, and I will not
apologize for that. I know your soul
is beautiful, despite your drinking and

your frightened little show of cynicism
and vulgarity, and this is all
I know or need to know.
    FLORENCE.
Please don't exasperate me beyond reason
by going on to further misquote Keats
on the identity of truth and beauty.
Keats was a lovesick imbecile like you.
It isn't me you love. It's her. Why can't
you just admit it and be done with it?
    CROOKES.
What is it, Florence? Why are you drinking so?
    FLORENCE.
Because I can no longer stomach this
grotesque pretense. It makes me sick.
I cannot do this any more. It's finished, Willy.
Pay the orchestra and go.
    CROOKES.
Florence, your work is far, far too important
to the history of mankind to give up now.
We owe it to posterity.
    FLORENCE.
Oh, bugger posterity. Will you not listen to me?
My work is flimflammery, flubdubbery,
prehensile scobjobbery. It is all one great
festering gob of snot and mollyclabber.
    CROOKES.
Snot and what?
    FLORENCE.
I'm a fake, Willy.
    CROOKES.
You are not a fake.
    FLORENCE.
Yes. I am.
    CROOKES.
No, you're not.

FLORENCE.
I am a fake. Why do you not believe me?
Listen, dolt. Shouldn't I be the one to know?
I am a fake, I tell you. Why would I claim
to be a fake if I was not one?
CROOKES.
Because you're drunk.
FLORENCE.
I'm drunk because I know I am a fake.
CROOKES.
You're drunk because you're terrified of what
you are, and the power God has given you.
I know what I have seen.
FLORENCE.
You don't know what you've seen. What have you seen?
CROOKES.
I've seen Katie King.
FLORENCE.
You have not seen Katie King.
You have seen me. I am Katie King.
CROOKES.
No you're not.
FLORENCE.
Listen to me, you gargantuan lip diddler,
you decorated Royal Society jackass.
I am Katie King, and she is me.
CROOKES.
She's not you. She's dead.
FLORENCE.
She is not dead, she is me.
CROOKES.
But I have touched her.
FLORENCE.
You have touched me.
CROOKES.
I have touched you, and I have touched her,

and believe me, I know the difference.
  FLORENCE.
No man ever born could tell the difference.
All cats are sluts in the dark.
When you were touching her, you were
touching me, and when you were touching
me, you were touching a whore.
  CROOKES.
Florence, stop it. This is lunacy.
  FLORENCE.
Of course it's lunacy. It is a thing
under the provenance of the moon
to love an imaginary dead girl.
I'm the Princess of Lunacy. Do you
not see how I'm imprisoned in the tower
of claptrap you have helped to build for me?
I'm suffocating in my cabinet coffin,
bound hand and foot, and I can only escape
in my underwear, and then only because
it gives you such great pleasure
to finger me in spooky candle light.
  CROOKES.
I have no idea what you're talking about.
I assure you, my motives are entirely pure.
  FLORENCE.
How can your motives be pure?
You're a man.
  CROOKES.
A married man.
  FLORENCE.
A married man. And who would you rather touch?
Your wife, or Katie King? Which supplies
the greater thrill? Come on. Be honest.
Truth, now. Beauty is truth, yes, Willy?
  CROOKES.
I cannot answer such a question.

FLORENCE.
Yes, since you'll take beauty over truth
and lie about it every time. Oh, what
can I do to make you understand?
     CROOKES.
I understand that you are making
no sense whatsoever. I personally
escort you to the cabinet. I personally
tie you up securely. And after each
manifestation, I personally check your
bonds, which are always utterly secure
and sealed with wax. With wax. They are
sealed with wax.
     FLORENCE.
Oh, wax, wax, wax, bugger wax.
Listen to me, you blockhead. I go into
the mystic cabinet, where I'm tied up.
When the cabinet is closed, I slip my bonds,
slither out of my dress, emerge in my
extremely fetching white undergarments
in the deep gloom of the séance, and
alikazam, I am Katie King, the girl
men love to touch.
     CROOKES.
No you're not.
     FLORENCE.
Do you not think I know who I am?
     CROOKES.
I think you have not the slightest
idea who you are. I think you are filled
with self-doubt and self-loathing.
I think the trance you enter into
frightens you, your powers terrify you,
and so you make up these degrading lies,
that you might flee from who you are.
I know that Katie King exists.

FLORENCE.
Listen to me. Is there ectoplasm in your ears?
I do not go into a trance. I have never
been in a trance in my life. What I do is,
I simply take off my dress, and walk about
in my underwear, making spooky noises.
I am an escape artist, and a ventriloquist,
and an actress, and a magician, and a
pathetic carnival confidence woman, and
if you were not so overwhelmed with lust
for my flesh, or rather, for the flesh of that
imaginary person Katie King, then you
would not be such a dunderhead as to
insist on stubbornly blinding yourself to
the simple fact of my utterly shameless and
infantile skullduggery. Why will you
not see it? You have made an investigation
into truth. Well, here is the truth.
The woman you profess to love does not
exist, and never did. It's all a lie.
Truth is a lie. There is no Katie King.
There is no Katie King.

CROOKES.
(Holding his head and moaning.)
Stop it. Stop it. Stop it. Why must you
torment me like this? Do you not understand?
I love you. I love you.

FLORENCE.
You are in love with a fictitious creation
made up entirely of my flesh and my
underwear. There is no her but me.
And I am merely a pretty and rather clever
little circus tart, who does a perilous
dance on a high wire between actress and
prostitute.

CROOKES.

I will not hear you speak this way.

I will not hear you desecrate a love

I know to be a pure and holy thing.

FLORENCE.

You love an illusion a whore has perpetrated

upon you. There is no Katie King. There is no

Katie King.

CROOKES.

(Grabbing her by the shoulders and shaking her.)

Shut up. Shut up. Shut up. Shut up. Shut up.

FLORENCE.

Yes, kill me. Why don't you kill me? Then

you can hold a séance and communicate

with my departed spirit. I'm sure I'll

be much easier to manage when I'm dead.

CROOKES.

(Letting her go.)

I'm sorry. I'm sorry. But when you fall into

these dark moods you drive me half insane.

I am not some credulous old woman.

I am the scientist who invented

the Crookes tube.

FLORENCE.

Bugger the Crookes tube.

CROOKES.

I am well respected in the realm of physics.

In physics, damn it. I am not

anybody's dupe. I am a celebrated

investigator into truth, and I have come

more and more of late to understand that

when we lumber into the séance dragging with us

the burden of our contempt, we kill the very

phenomena we are attempting to

investigate. The presence of the observer

inevitably alters and pollutes

the experiment beyond all possibility
of redemption. Of course we cannot prove
these matters true. They will not manifest
themselves in an atmosphere of disbelief.
This thrives on ambiguity, not because
it is a lie, but precisely because of the
manner in which it is true.
       FLORENCE.
You must get over this sickness of believing, Willy.
There is no more believing in this place.
Your beloved Katie King is dead.
Or, worse than dead, she never was alive.
Mourn her, accept it, and go on
It is the only way.

(He sits at the table, holding his head.)

       CROOKES.
Oh, if you only knew what you are. If you
only knew what you are.
       FLORENCE.
I know what I am, my dear. I know too well.
And so, I think, in your heart, do you.

(She touches his hair with some tenderness.)

       CROOKES.
But Florence, listen to me. If you are
the charlatan you say you are, then why
would you be trying to convince me of it?
Why not go on deceiving me?
       FLORENCE.
Because you love me, or you think you do,
and yet you don't, and yet the ambiguity
distresses me so deeply, I look into your
eyes and see the adoration, and know

it is a lie you love—I am a whore, Willy.
I am just not a very good one. And
I am sorry to have hurt you. But you
cannot let another create reality for you.
That way madness lies, or worse, love.
Katie King is dead. Katie King is dead.

(Sound of the clock ticking. She takes his face in both her hands and very tenderly kisses him on the lips. Then we hear the cabinet door creaking open, and KATIE KING steps out. She is a pretty young woman who looks remarkably like FLORENCE in her underwear.)

KATIE.
She's right, you know, Willy. I'm quite dead.
CROOKES.
(Looking up at her.)
Katie?
FLORENCE.
See there? Even she agrees with me. Tell him.
KATIE.
I'm dead. Or I would be except I never was alive.
I don't exist. I am her. She is me. We are
the same flesh and blood apparition.
CROOKES.
No you're not.
KATIE.
Yes I am. Trust me, Willy. I am her. I'm her.
CROOKES.
But how can you be her when you are there,
and she is clearly here?
KATIE.
Well, then, if that's the case, we must change places.
Ready?
FLORENCE.
Absolutely.

(They make a great show of changing places.)

KATIE.
(Holding up her arms like a magician's assistant.)
Ta dahhhhhh!
There. You see? Now she is there and I
am here, the both of us, which means that we
are obviously the same girl. Certainly
no reasonable man could doubt the evidence
of his own eyes, even a scientist.
CROOKES.
But I am seeing you.
KATIE.
Exactly.
CROOKES.
And you are here simultaneously.
KATIE.
Only because we're the same person.
FLORENCE.
And also, I am somewhere else entirely.
CROOKES.
You are here, and so is she.
FLORENCE.
No, actually, I am tied up in the cabinet.
CROOKES.
How can you be tied up in the cabinet
when you are here beside me?
FLORENCE.
Obviously I can't. Which proves that I am
not here at all. So I must be in the cabinet.
KATIE.
Very good, Florence, for a girl from Hackney.
He has no answer to that one, does he?
You have utterly mystified a distinguished
pillar of the scientific community.
If I were real, I would kiss you.

CROOKES.
I think I must be going mad.
I cannot understand this.
What is happening here?
FLORENCE.
It's simple, really, Willy. Before I
discovered Katie, I was sitting about
gathering barnacles in Hackney and
suffering through an excruciatingly morbid
adolescence, fighting off the attentions
of red faced young men with large buttocks
and the intelligence of fungus, and now
and then enjoying the stray vision, or
hysterical attack of nerves and thereby
at least granting myself the opportunity
of experiencing an orgasm or two.
And then one day Katie King began
to manifest herself, and suddenly
I was entertaining the Earl of Caithness and the
Duke of Bedford's brother in the parlor,
among the aspidistras and the mildewed
antimacassars and being invited by
fantastically wealthy men to sail to Paris
for the benefit of my health, which in fact
was excellent.
CROOKES.
But she did manifest herself. You've just
admitted that. So Katie King is real.
FLORENCE.
I suppose in the beginning
I might have believed there really was
such a person as she. But soon I knew
the truth. The truth is that truth is a lie.
CROOKES.
BUT SHE IS HERE.

FLORENCE.
Well, of course she is. Where else would she be?
KATIE.
Of course I'm here. Except when I'm gone.
But then of course Florence is here,
because Florence is always here, where
else would she be? So I'm even here
when I'm not here. I'm even more talented
that I thought I was. Oh, don't look so sad, Willy.
We have had some good times, have we not?
Remember the séance when I insisted
on tying you up and covering you with
a table cloth, then ordered you to be
as still as a dead man's dick
while a chair full of musical instruments
was balanced on top of your head?
Wasn't that fun?
FLORENCE.
Your sense of humor was always one
of your best qualities, Katie. Along with
your figure, of course. You do look
lovely in my underwear, don't I?
KATIE.
Yes, I must admit, we do. And Willy,
what about the time I allowed you
to feel the large hole in the back of
my head, and told you I had been
in such a hurry to materialize for you,
that I had forgotten to finish myself?
FLORENCE.
Yes. We have always had a rather large
hole in our head. And we have forgotten
to finish ourself. We left finishing school
before we had even properly begun.
But I am now going to remedy that.
I've determined at last to finish myself,

once and for all.

CROOKES.

What do you mean?

FLORENCE.

I mean that I think I am nearly done here,
so I am going now.

CROOKES.

Going where?

FLORENCE.

Going somewhere else, of course. Where
would I go but somewhere else? The only
other place I could possibly go is here, and
I'm already here, or nowhere, and if I were
to go nowhere, then I would still be here,
for this is as close to nowhere
as any girl has ever got, I think.

CROOKES.

You can't go. What will you do?

FLORENCE.

Do? What will I do? Well, I suppose
I could sell my flesh to sailors, men
more ignorant than you but far less stupid.
Yes, I think I am going somewhere
to make men pay to touch me.

CROOKES.

Florence—

FLORENCE.

I'm sorry Willy, but I am no longer able
to hear you, for I have already begun
to dematerialized into the ether.
Alikazam. Sis boom bah. Shuttlecocks.

(FLORENCE walks into the cabinet and closes the door.)

CROOKES.

Florence? You have simply walked into

the cabinet. You're not going to find any
sailors in there. Florence?
    KATIE.
Ah, Willy. Alone at last.
    CROOKES.
Florence? Hello?

(He knocks on the cabinet door.)

    KATIE.
Will you leave poor Florence alone?
Florence has simply wandered off into
the effluvium of more conventional whoredom.
Whilst—lucky me—I am left here with you.
I know you have always desired me.
    CROOKES.
Florence? Are you all right in there?
May I get you anything? Would you like
some windmill cookies and a spot
of LeFanu's green tea?
    KATIE.
You don't want Florence, Willy. You want me.
It has always been me you really wanted,
and Florence has always known that.
She has been merely the fleshly vessel
I have crossed over the waters in.
    CROOKES.
Florence?
    KATIE.
Oh, bugger Florence. Florence has gone
to the Great Gromboolian Plain, but I
shall always be with you, Willy Crookes.
And I shall never die, for I am already dead.
    CROOKES.
Florence? I am opening this cabinet. Florence?
Hello? I am opening this cabinet now.

I hope you are decent.
    KATIE.
Florence has never been decent in her life.
She's from Hackney.
    CROOKES.
Florence?
*(He opens the cabinet. Sound of it creaking. The cabinet is
    empty.)*
Florence? Where are you? Where is she?
What have you done with Florence?
    KATIE.
You may touch me now if you like.
You may place your fingers reverently
upon my tremulous white faux-virgin limbs.
We shall rub ectoplasm over one another's
naked flesh and fornicate like frenzied
rabbits on the green baize table.
Phantom love is the best love, you know.
In fact, it is the only love. Touch me.
    CROOKES.
No. I can't.
    KATIE.
Oh, but the dead so long to be touched.
Especially the imaginary dead.
Touch me. Touch my flesh.
Do you fear that your hand will
go entirely through me?
    CROOKES.
Where has she gone? You must tell me
where she has gone.
    KATIE.
She has escaped into the mirrors.
It is all done with mirrors, you see.
It is all mirrors and carousel horses.
But since I have the distinct advantage
of never having existed in the first place,

I have nowhere to go. I'm yours forever.

(She closes the closet door, which creaks and bangs.)

CROOKES.
Mine? You're not mine. How can you
be mine? You're a spiritual manifestation.
     KATIE.
No, I am that most seductive and yet most
unsatisfying of all human objects:
I am a work of art. I am just real
enough to make you miserable forever.
A thing of beauty is a kind of hell,
the poet said, before he died a virgin.
Now come and touch me, Willy, before I
grow so annoyed that I begin to haunt you
with a vengeance. Trust me, you do not want a girl
to be annoyed when she is haunting you.
Willy? Touch me. Please just touch me once.
Touch me, and then, if you don't like it—
(He reaches out his hand to touch just between her breasts.
     She holds his hand in both of hers and presses it to her
     flesh.)
There we are. All better now. All better.
There's a good boy. Isn't that better? Yes.
I can feel the ectoplasm flowing. Now both hands.

(He looks at her. The sound of the ticking clock. Then there is
     a pounding from the inside of the cabinet.)

FLORENCE.
(From within the cabinet.)
Willy? Let me out. I've changed my mind.
It's dark in here. I do not like this place.
I will pretend. I will pretend that I am anyone
you want. Oh, Willy? Willy? Let me out.

It's like a coffin in here. Willy? Will?
I miss you.
(CROOKES reaches out both hands to touch the breasts of KATIE KING. FLORENCE continues pounding from within the cabinet.)
Willy? I love you. Can you hear me? Willy?
I love you. I love you.

(The light fades on them and goes out. Sound of the pounding in the darkness.)

END OF PLAY

THE DEAD WIFE

CHARACTERS

Laura, a woman in her mid-twenties
Maud, a woman of thirty

SETTING

A bedroom. Night.

THE DEAD WIFE

(Lights up on LAURA, a young woman in her mid-twenties, who sits on a bed, wearing a white nightgown. Standing nearby is MAUD, a woman of thirty, who wears a black nightgown. We can hear the ticking of a clock.)

LAURA. It's my wedding night, and I would very much appreciate it if you would please go away and leave me alone now.

MAUD. Ah, the wedding night. Yes, I remember that. He is very good at wedding nights, I can tell you from experience.

LAURA. I don't want to hear about your wedding night.

MAUD. You must be very proud of the extraordinarily privileged position you will soon find yourself in. You are about to be violated by one of the most celebrated icons of civilization as we know it.

LAURA. Of course I'm proud to be his wife. Why should I not be proud? His exploits upon the field of battle are justly celebrated.

MAUD. Yes. A hero is always the best killer. And having grown up, as you did, among the genteel poor and the conventionally stupid, to actually be permitted to enter as a character, even a minor character, into the epic of a genuine hero of our time, it is such an honor, such a spectacular opportunity, that sometimes I expect you must be simply overwhelmed by your good fortune, and your unworthiness for such a position. And

121

I speak to you as one who now merely steps out of the water naked, whispering, in your dreams.

LAURA. I do not feel unworthy, but I feel fortunate. And I feel that this marriage will be a good thing for him as well as for me.

MAUD. And on what evidence do you base this optimistic prognostication?

LAURA. I consulted the tarot cards before I agreed to marry him, and they told me this union would be a great success.

MAUD. The cards told you, did they?

LAURA. Yes. The cards told me.

MAUD. The first time you asked?

LAURA. Not the first time, but the second.

MAUD. Yes. It is extremely important in matters of life and death to keep annoying the oracle until you get the prediction you want.

LAURA. Could you please go away? I really hope you don't intend to observe at first hand the consummation of our marriage.

MAUD. Oh, but I think I could not possibly refrain from watching.

LAURA. Have you no decency? Have you no sense of shame whatsoever?

MAUD. Shame? You speak to me of decency and shame? Why don't you ask your husband about decency and shame? Ask him if he feels the slightest bit of shame when he thinks of me, why don't you?

LAURA. I don't want him to think about you. I have striven mightily to help him forget about you. I think in fact that has been my chief occupation.

MAUD. And have you succeeded?

LAURA. Yes. I think so. He had already made some progress. He put away all your photographs.

MAUD. But one rainy day you found them.

LAURA. Yes.

MAUD. Packed in a trunk, in the attic.

LAURA. Yes. I was doing some housecleaning. I was not snooping.

MAUD. Well, of course you were snooping. You are the new wife, it is your duty to be snooping. I am quite touched that he could not bring himself to destroy them.

LAURA. I have done my best to accept the fact that he must have loved you very much.

MAUD. Oh, yes. He must have.

LAURA. And I am not by nature a jealous person, or a fanciful person.

MAUD. He must have. Yes.

LAURA. And yet, try as I might, I cannot seem to get you out of my brain.

MAUD. Is that where I am? In your brain?

LAURA. Of course it is. You're not real. You're quite dead.

MAUD. Well, perhaps not quite. But you love him very much, do you?

LAURA. Of course I do. I love him desperately.

MAUD. And do you believe that he loves you very much?

LAURA. I have every reason to hope that he does.

MAUD. Yes. You have every reason to hope.

LAURA. Why do you look at me with such contempt? It isn't my fault that you're dead. Don't you want him to be happy? Don't you want him to find love again?

MAUD. To find love again. To find love. And you, of course, in your vast fund of life experience, are a great authority upon love, are you?

LAURA. At least I am capable of it.

MAUD. And you believe I was not?

LAURA. I can't say that. I don't know. All I can say is that if you truly loved him, you would go away and let us alone.

MAUD. I will tell you about love, my dear. Love is the most exquisite form of cannibalism. To love is to see your own death in the eyes of another. God's world is made of this. The animals devour one another, and we devour the animals, and when the animals are gone, we devour each other, and this, for want of a better definition, we call love.

LAURA. Love is not anything like that. Will you please go away? He'll be here any moment now.

MAUD. Do you like this place, child?

LAURA. I love this place.

MAUD. You love the weather here?

LAURA. No. Not the weather. I hope I am not required to love the weather as well. The fact is, it rains entirely too much in this place, and yet everything here seems to be dying. Why do you suppose that is?

MAUD. You are a very stupid girl, you know.

LAURA. I am not stupid at all. I was the smartest girl in my class. I always got the highest marks.

MAUD. And yet you chose to be this man's wife.

LAURA. Yes. I chose. I had a choice, and I chose. I chose what you chose.

MAUD. Yes, and look how well it has worked out for me.

LAURA. I am not going to sit here and be insulted by my husband's dead wife on my wedding night.

MAUD. Look at yourself. Look at yourself in the mirror.

LAURA. I don't like mirrors.

MAUD. I have gathered that you don't. You've covered up all the mirrors in the house, as if somebody has died.

LAURA. Somebody has died. You have died.

MAUD. Are you afraid of your own reflection?

LAURA. I'm afraid I'll look in the mirror and see you.

MAUD. You could look in the mirror and see worse.

LAURA. I don't want to look in the mirror.

MAUD. How can you let him touch you?

LAURA. Why shouldn't I let him touch me? You let him touch you.

MAUD. Oh, yes, I let him touch me. Yes, I did let him touch me. And in the end, I died for it.

LAURA. You died in a random act of violence.

MAUD. Human violence is never random. I was murdered.

LAURA. By a burglar.

MAUD. No.

LAURA. By a madman.

MAUD. Well, that's closer. In fact, I was murdered by my husband.

LAURA. That's absurd.

MAUD. Yes, but like many absurd things, absolutely true.

LAURA. This is rubbish. I am not going to listen to this.

MAUD. You had better listen to me, dear, because the dead also have a tale to tell, although we murdered often have our mouths stuffed with clotted rue to shut us up, but still we find a way to jabber, jabber, when we have something important to relate to the living. A man is like a prison, dear, he is like a spider crawling on your face, he is like a bath in honey, first sweet, then cloying, then it begins to choke you as your head goes under, and you suffocate and die. I remember counting the number of times the knife went in, one for each kiss I gave him on our wedding night.

LAURA. Shut up. Go away. You're horrible. You are not wanted here.

MAUD. I know. I know. I was you once. But nobody warned me. Of course if they had, I would not have listened. I entered into this as ignorantly as you. What skills did I bring with me to my marriage? I was beautiful of course, for what that's worth, and I had a good heart.

LAURA. You were cruel. You were insane.

MAUD. I was charming company. I had a sense of humor. Both men and women adored me. I loved my children. The killer has them now. Which will die next, I wonder? Because violence is not a thing which stops, no, violence must eat and eat and eat again, it is not, cannot ever become satisfied.

LAURA. Stop it. I will not listen. I will not.

MAUD. I speak only the truth. The beast in his heart, which once propelled the knife into my flesh, still lives. The killer sees through different eyes. He must search always for a fresh victim. In her dreams my little girl will see the ritual cutting of her mother's throat, like the blooding of a pig.

LAURA. Why are you doing this?

MAUD. I've been watching him closely since my death, and I believe he has come to the realization that one of the great fringe benefits of being wealthy is that a man is permitted at least one free murder, or two, if the killer is both rich and well known. Lovers and parents are popular choices for this honor, but wives are the preferred victims. It had not occurred to me before my murder that what is relevant in such matters is not that a large, strong man with a sharp knife has butchered the woman who once gave birth to his children. What is relevant is his value as a kind of universal symbol of virility, of conquest, of surrogate power or revenge for those who cheer him on faithfully, his admirers, his accomplices. We worship at the feet of heroes. We worship them and give ourselves to them. We do not love the gentle or the shy, we love the violent who betray us, beat us if we object, and then exercise the ultimate control by slaughtering us. It is the final act of love, the ritual evisceration of the beloved object. It is the most intimate act of passion of which the hero is capable.

LAURA. I know why you're doing this. It's because you're jealous. You're jealous of our happiness, his and mine. You could not be happy yourself, and so you wish to draw me into your web of unhappiness.

MAUD. Money makes truth, but violence is our god. This is why you worship him. You are drawn to violence, to his capacity for violence.

LAURA. I am disgusted by violence. Do you think I wish to be killed? To be abused? Do you think I crave abuse?

MAUD. Sometimes I watch you when you have just emerged naked from the bath, and I imagine how one day he will dismember you. I pity you, but I see the glassy look in your eyes, and recognize in you my own stupid coma of adulation, the fascination of the lamb for the butcher.

LAURA. Why don't you haunt him? If he is the one who killed you, why not haunt him instead of tormenting me?

MAUD. I have attempted to haunt him, but he has become

remarkably good at shutting me out, mostly with liquor, drugs and golf. I fear that I am fading now from his minuscule brain. All that I have been or done drains out in a puddle on the stones. The sad truth is that some people are just too stupid to haunt.

LAURA. If you have such contempt for him then why did you marry him in the first place?

MAUD. Because I was not dead then. Then I was you, or something very like you. I was, in short, alive and stupid. Death really opens your eyes.

LAURA. He loves me. That is really what you can't accept.

MAUD. The real death is to be frozen into a symbol. This way they never have to look at you again. They need not see you crying, or giving birth, or comforting your children while Daddy goes berserk.

LAURA. He does not go berserk. His children love him.

MAUD. Well, of course they love him. At least, they want to love him. As you do. They must love somebody, mustn't they? And it is much easier to cheer our hero on when we are not ourselves actually being at the moment splattered in the face with the gore of his human sacrifices. But that is not the worst. The worst is that they are forgetting me. My children are forgetting me. They try not to, but already I am blurring like water colors in the rain.

LAURA. What do you want from me? Do you want me to pity you? All right. I pity you. You were murdered horribly. You have lost your life. I pity you for that. But now you must leave me alone and let the living get on with their lives.

MAUD. You pull your ignorance over your head like a winter quilt. You wear dark spectacles and are as blind as I was. He is a master of making people blind. A hero is a person whose capacity for violence is unlimited. And by definition all that a hero does is good. His lies make truth. And money makes truth. And all who deny this holy truth are the enemy. And of course a hero also has enemies, and many of those who hate him and wish to kill him in fact envy him and want to be him, long to possess the stupid ruthlessness to murder their own beloved. It is especially fascinating for me, as a dead person, to watch the army of sycophantic ghouls he drags around behind him, rich, carnivorous whores with law degrees, their brains made of lies and excrement. They vomit chunks of body parts and excrement out on the marble floor and men take pictures. All who take part in this ritual creep out into the daylight, if at all, blinking and covered in shit. History is a shopping list of murderers, and the most spectacularly successful of all the butchers become gods. I was sacrificed naked to the god of copulation.

LAURA. I will not listen to this filth. Just tell me what you want. What do you want from me? Did you come here to kill me, or merely to drive me insane, like you? Do you hate me so much that you would deprive your children of a second mother?

MAUD. I might easily hate you. You took my children, and still take them.

LAURA. I am good to your children. Your children love me.

MAUD. You will watch them grow up into twisted things without me. They will pretend they believe he didn't kill me, but in their hearts, they will know. They will see him slaughtering me, like a mad play in a dark theatre, the same scene, over and over, until they are quite mad. In the end, they will despise him, and they will despise you, and you will despise him, but by then it will be too late. They will be utterly lost. Or perhaps he will kill them first.

LAURA. I will not despise him.

MAUD. In your soul, I think you already despise him.

LAURA. That's a lie.

MAUD. It's not a lie. It's why you can see me.

LAURA. I cannot see you.

MAUD. His children will make him pay, so he will kill them.

LAURA. He would never hurt his children.

MAUD. Just his wife.

LAURA. He would never hurt me.

MAUD. When he looks at them, he will see me, and when they look at you, they will see my ripped open flesh. I hope

there is a proper hell for him somewhere. I must fight the urge
to pity you. I think it's pity that has been my downfall. And it
is out of this lingering perverse sense of identification with
the other that our hatred grows, and rots, exploding finally
into the bloody summer night like the one I was butchered on.
The dead are confused by this. To love the other, to possess
the other, to be the other, to kill the other, is to murder ourselves.
To unite one's soul with the killer's soul and not the victim's:
this is what the violent have taught us.

LAURA. Listen. He is coming. He is coming now. You
must go away.

MAUD. There were candles burning all around my gaping
corpse.

LAURA. You must not be here when he comes.

MAUD. You must save yourself and my children.

LAURA. How can I save myself? You couldn't.

MAUD. I tried.

LAURA. No, I think you liked it. I think you wanted to be
murdered. You liked making up after a quarrel. The more violent the quarrel, the more wonderful the making up. He told
me that. I think fear was a part of your fascination with him.

MAUD. So you blame me for my own murder? This is
what he and his ghouls are teaching my children, that I am
responsible for my own murder, that in fact I must have stabbed
myself sixty-eight times. They whisper that I deserved to die.
They whisper it should have been a privilege to be murdered
by such a glorious hero of our time.

LAURA. Stop it. He is coming. He is coming. You will
drive me mad. Lately I have been dreaming of your naked
corpse, surrounded by candles. Only sometimes it is not you.
Sometimes it is his daughter. And sometimes it is me. I am the
dead girl lying amid the lighted candles.

MAUD. If you cannot save yourself, then at least save my
children.

LAURA. How can I save them?

MAUD. I have brought a wedding present for you.

LAURA. A present?

MAUD. Yes. *(She produces something wrapped in a scarlet cloth.)* Here. A gift upon your wedding night, with the warmest compliments of the dead wife.

(MAUD holds out the object to LAURA.)

LAURA. What is this?

MAUD. They never found the murder weapon, did they?

LAURA. No.

MAUD. Take this, with my love.

(LAURA takes the object, and opens up the scarlet cloth. In it is a blood stained knife.)

LAURA. This is madness.

MAUD. Violence is madness. Love is madness. This is merely a fashioned object. It may be used for good or ill.

LAURA. Where did you get this?

MAUD. He buried it in the woods.

LAURA. What do you expect me to do with this?

MAUD. He's coming now. He is on the steps now. He is coming to his wedding bed. He wants your flesh now. He wants to violate your flesh, to enter into you and possess you. And at that moment, when the animal is most vulnerable, that is when you must do it.

LAURA. I can't.

MAUD. You want to.

LAURA. I don't want to.

MAUD. Oh, yes. Yes you do. Very much. Very much. For the last part of the ritual, the final act of worship we perform for our beloved, the hero, is to kill him.

(LAURA looks at the knife. Sound of heavy footsteps coming up the stairs. The light fades on them and goes out.)

END OF PLAY

WONDERS OF
THE INVISIBLE WORLD
REVEALED

"People down the village heard shouts and shrieks, and looking up the street saw the Coach and Horses violently firing out its humanity. They saw Mrs. Hall fall down and Mr. Teddy Henfrey jump to avoid tumbling over her, and then they heard the frightful screams of Millie, who, emerging suddenly from the kitchen at the noise of the tumult, had come upon the headless stranger from behind." —H.G. Wells

CHARACTERS:

Millie, a young housemaid
Griffin, a man in his forties

SETTING:

A parlor at the Coach and Horses, an inn in Sussex,
towards the end of the nineteenth century.
Just an arm chair for Griffin will do.

WONDERS OF THE
INVISIBLE WORLD REVEALED

(Sound of a ticking clock. Lights up on a parlor at the Coach and Horses, an inn in Sussex. GRIFFIN sits in a chair, his face wrapped and concealed entirely in bandages. His hair is a somewhat disorderly dark shock emerging from the bandages rather like an unfortunate wig, which is of course what it is. He wears blue tinted glasses, and gloves on his hands, so that every part of his body is concealed either by clothing, gloves, bandages or glasses. He is drinking Scotch. MILLIE, a young housemaid, stands there looking at him. Shadows of crackling fire. Ticking clock.)

MILLIE. Will there be anything else, sir?

GRIFFIN. Will there be anything else?

MILLIE. Will you be wanting anything else tonight, sir?

GRIFFIN. Will I be wanting anything else? You're asking me to predict the future, are you?

MILLIE. No, sir. I just—

GRIFFIN. Do you imagine that I possess some sort of time machine, that I have the ability to venture forth into the future so as to be able to know with some degree of certainty what, if anything, I will be wanting tonight, or tomorrow night, or ten years from tonight, or even if I shall be alive then, or ten minutes from now, or for that matter if you shall be alive ten minutes from now to get it for me, if in fact you are actually capable of getting what I want. Can you get what I want?

MILLIE. I don't know, sir.

GRIFFIN. Why not?

MILLIE. Because I don't know what it is, sir. I can't get you what you want if I don't know what it is, and I can't know what it is if you don't tell me, and you can't tell me if you don't know, so perhaps I should not have asked the question in the first place, sir. Will that be all, sir? No, wait, let me rephrase that, what I mean to say is, may I be excused now?

GRIFFIN. Excused? May you be excused? Do you think it is my business to be excusing you? I am not a priest, you know. I hope you have not come here under the mistaken impression that I am in any way prepared to exonerate you for your sins, I hope you have not come here looking for some sort of absolution, because I can't do that. Have you come here seeking forgiveness for your sins?

MILLIE. I came here because it's my job, sir. *(Pause.)* May I go now, sir?

GRIFFIN. What's your name?

MILLIE. My name, sir?

GRIFFIN. Yes, your name. That's not an impossibly difficult question, is it? Don't you know your name?

MILLIE. Yes, sir.

GRIFFIN. Well, what is it? I hope I shall not be forced to guess. Is it a secret name, like Rumplestiltskin?

MILLIE. My name is not Rumplestiltskin, sir. It's Millie.

GRIFFIN. Millie?

MILLIE. Yes, sir.

GRIFFIN. Have you ever thought of changing it to Rumplestiltskin?

MILLIE. No, sir. If that's all, sir—

GRIFFIN. Did I say that was all?

MILLIE. No, sir.

GRIFFIN. Then it's not all, is it?

MILLIE. I suppose not, sir.

(Pause.)

GRIFFIN. You're fidgeting, Millie.

MILLIE. No, I'm not, sir.

GRIFFIN. Don't tell me you're not fidgeting. I know fidgeting when I see fidgeting, I've seen plenty of young girls fidget in my presence, and let me tell you, Millie, and I say this with absolute confidence, you are one intensely fidgeting little person. Now, why are you fidgeting?

MILLIE. I don't know, sir.

GRIFFIN. Is it perhaps because I make you just a bit uncomfortable, Millie? Can it be that I make you just a wee bit nervous? Do I frighten you?

MILLIE. No, sir.

GRIFFIN. I don't frighten you?

MILLIE. No, sir.

GRIFFIN. Then what the hell are you looking at me like that for?

MILLIE. Like what, sir?

GRIFFIN. Like I've just eaten the baby with relish and mustard. Because I haven't eaten the baby, Millie.

MILLIE. I know that, sir.

GRIFFIN. You know I haven't eaten the baby? How do you know I haven't eaten the baby? How can you be certain I haven't eaten the baby?

MILLIE. Because we have no baby, sir. In this house, sir. There is no baby.

GRIFFIN. Of course we have no baby. And do you know why we have no baby, Millie? Because I've eaten it.

MILLIE. Now you're making fun of me, sir.

GRIFFIN. I'm making fun of you? The baby has just been devoured before your very eyes and all you can think about is whether or not I'm making fun of you? I must tell you, Millie, I think that's a very selfish position for you to take. It's really unworthy of you. What's the matter? What the hell do you think you're looking at? Have you never before set eyes upon a man entirely wrapped in bandages?

MILLIE. No, sir. I haven't. I'm sorry, sir.

GRIFFIN. Why are you sorry? Are you sorry that I'm wrapped in bandages? Or are you sorry that you're looking at me? Or are you merely sorry that I've caught you looking at me?

MILLIE. I'm sorry if I've offended you, sir.

GRIFFIN. If you're curious about the damned bandages, then why don't you just ask me how I got them? Don't you want to ask me?

MILLIE. No, sir.

GRIFFIN. Why not? Don't you care?

MILLIE. It's none of my business, sir.

GRIFFIN. I didn't ask you if it was any of your business. Of course it's none of your business. You're a servant. Nothing is any of your business. I asked you if you cared why I am wrapped up in these bandages. Are you telling me you don't care, or are you telling me you wish I'd go and stick my head under an omnibus?

MILLIE. I don't know what I'm telling you, sir. May I please go now, sir?

GRIFFIN. If you want to know, just ask me. As me why I have these bandages. Go on. Ask me. Ask me.

MILLIE. Why do you have those bandages, sir?

GRIFFIN. Can't you guess?

MILLIE. No, sir, I can't guess.

GRIFFIN. Oh, come on, Millie. You can guess. You're not a complete imbecile, even if you are a common housemaid. I can tell you're not entirely imbecilic by the way you look at me, the way a mongoose looks at a cobra. Guess why I have these bandages. Go on. Guess.

MILLIE. I don't want to guess.

GRIFFIN. Nobody cares what you want, Millie. Guess. Guess why the new lodger at the Coach and Horses in the darkest and most abysmal arse end of picturesque and moldy, smuggly, swamp-infested Sussex appears to be entirely wrapped in bandages. Guess.

MILLIE. Was it some sort of an accident, sir?

GRIFFIN. An accident? You believe in accidents, do you, Millie?

MILLIE. Of course I do.

GRIFFIN. So you take the philosophical position that God is not all powerful?

MILLIE. Of course not, sir.

GRIFFIN. Well, you can't have it both ways, Millie. Either you believe that God is all powerful, and there are no accidents, because God is the cause of all things happening, or else you believe that there are accidents, and therefore God is not all powerful. So which is it, Millie? Which do you believe?

MILLIE. I believe that something has happened to you, sir, which has made you very unhappy.

GRIFFIN. Unhappy? You think I'm unhappy?

MILLIE. I think you must be a very unhappy person, sir, or else you wouldn't be wasting so much of your time bullying a poor servant girl.

(Pause.)

GRIFFIN. Yes. I suppose it was an accident.

(Pause.)

MILLIE. What kind of accident?

GRIFFIN. A metaphysical accident. Do you know what that means, Millie?

MILLIE. No, sir.

GRIFFIN. Well, I don't either. I thought I did once, but now I don't. *(Pause.)* Why do you look at me that way? You have a rather disturbing gaze, Millie, did you know that? You look at me as if—as if I interested you. But I don't interest you, do I, Millie?

MILLIE. Yes, sir. You do interest me.

GRIFFIN. Why do I interest you?

MILLIE. You're different.

GRIFFIN. Different that what?

MILLIE. Different than anything.

GRIFFIN. Yes. I'm different, all right. Because of my—accident. Because of my—affliction. My—deformity.

MILLIE. It's not just that. It isn't just the bandages. It's also the way you are. The way you talk. The way you don't talk. The fact that you've filled up your room almost entirely with bottles. I've never seen so many bottles in my life. And your constant preoccupation. Your complete lack of civility. Your perfectly horrible temper. There's just something immensely odd about you. It's as if you had some terrible secret.

GRIFFIN. Of course I have a secret. This is England. Everybody has a secret. Even you. You have a secret. Don't you have a secret?

MILLIE. No, sir. *(Pause.)* Well, perhaps I do. I mean, nothing in particular, so much as a rather small number of private things which would probably be of no significance to anybody else were they known, but which—

GRIFFIN. I'll tell you my secret if you'll tell me yours.

MILLIE. But I've just said that I don't think I have any particular—

GRIFFIN. One secret. Any secret. Just one. I'll trade you, Millie. Your secret for mine. Come on. I can see you're dying to know. One secret of mine for one secret of yours. Is it a bargain?

(Pause.)

MILLIE. You first.

GRIFFIN. No, you first.

MILLIE. No. You first, or it's no bargain.

GRIFFIN. But why must I go first? After all, you're the servant, aren't you?

MILLIE. Yes, that's why.

GRIFFIN. You don't trust me, Millie. You don't trust me to keep my end of the bargain. Good for you. But are you absolutely certain that you want to know my secret? Because you must take into consideration, Millie, that once a person has revealed a secret to another person, nothing between them can ever be the same. Revelations create a kind of terrible intimacy, a kind of nakedness, as it were. Once one has stood naked before another, the universe is altered irrevocably, as by a kind of death. Revelations alter everything that comes after.

MILLIE Nothing comes after Revelations, sir. Revelations is the last book.

(Pause.)

GRIFFIN. This is true. This is true. So you're certain you want to know my secret, then?

MILLIE. Yes. I am. I'm certain. It's none of my business, but I am certain. I want to know.

GRIFFIN. What a brave girl you are, Millie. I like that. I like that very much. I am so pleased by your boldness and your unexpected cleverness that I shall accept the terms of your bargain and tell you my secret. Are you ready?

MILLIE. I'm ready.

GRIFFIN. All right. My secret, Millie, is that I'm invisible.

MILLIE. I beg your pardon?

GRIFFIN. I'm invisible. I am entirely invisible.

MILLIE. Invisible?

GRIFFIN. Yes. I am an invisible man.

MILLIE. An invisible man?

GRIFFIN. That's me.

MILLIE. You're invisible?

GRIFFIN. Absolutely.

MILLIE. No you're not.

GRIFFIN. Yes I am.

MILLIE. But you're not. Invisible means you can't be seen.

GRIFFIN. That's correct.

MILLIE. But I can see you.

GRIFFIN. Can you?

MILLIE. Of course I can.

GRIFFIN. Are you certain?

MILLIE. Yes I'm certain. I'm looking right at you, and there you are.

GRIFFIN. But are you certain it's me you're seeing?

MILLIE. Well, if it isn't you, who is it?

GRIFFIN. And if it is me, who isn't it?

MILLIE. What?

GRIFFIN. What you think you're looking at, Millie, is no more who I am than, say, your flesh, the warm pink wrapper of flesh which covers your meat, bones and innards, which covers your feet, your legs, your stomach, your back, your shoulders, your face, your breasts, the nipples of your breasts—this outer shell which you are looking at, Millie, this pathetic husk, is no more who I am than your flesh is who you are. You are no more the flesh of your breasts than I am this ridiculous pile of bandages and clothing I have wrapped around myself. You must never mistake the bundle of dirty laundry I carry around with me like a walking clothesline for who I am, Millie. For who I am, in reality, is an invisible man. *(Pause.)* What is it, Millie? Are you ill? You're not going to vomit, are you?

MILLIE. I don't think you should be speaking to me about my breasts, sir.

GRIFFIN. But, Millie, if I don't, who will?

MILLIE. I hope nobody will.

GRIFFIN. Never?

MILLIE. I think I should go now, sir.

GRIFFIN. And yet you don't go. Because you don't want to go. You want to see me, don't you? You want to see what an invisible man looks like. But you can't see me. And this troubles you. And I understand your feelings perfectly, Millie, because I also would very, very much like to see you.

MILLIE. You're looking right at me.

GRIFFIN. But am I seeing you?

MILLIE. You are unless you're blind.

GRIFFIN. Unless I'm blind. Yes.

MILLIE. Are you blind?

GRIFFIN. Am I blind? Well, that would depend, I suppose, on what you mean by blind.

MILLIE. You're not blind.

GRIFFIN. How do you know I'm not blind?

MILLIE. Because I've watched you go up and down the stairs.

GRIFFIN. Have you? Have you watched me?

MILLIE. Well, you watch me. I've seen you watching me. You watch me all the time. And all these bottles.

GRIFFIN. What about them? What have bottles got to do with it?

MILLIE. You couldn't very well be messing about with all these very peculiar oddly shaped scientific experimental laboratory bottles all day every day if you were blind, now, could you? You'd be knocking over bottles left and right. But you never break one of them, do you?

GRIFFIN. I have broken a bottle or two, in my time, Millie, I assure you. But not many. And yet one might still be blind and yet not break bottles. Some of the blind are very agile, I think. Some of the blind are as graceful as ballerinas.

MILLIE. If you're blind, then what do you want with all these bottles?

GRIFFIN. With these bottles I make myself invisible.

MILLIE. Why?

GRIFFIN. Why?

MILLIE. Why would anybody want to be invisible?

GRIFFIN. Oh, for any number of reasons.

MILLIE. What reasons?

GRIFFIN. Well, um, for example, an invisible man can steal fruit.

MILLIE. Steal fruit? You want to be invisible so you can steal fruit?

GRIFFIN. It's just an example.

MILLIE. But wouldn't people see the fruit? Flying through the air?

GRIFFIN. Well, yes, but—

MILLIE. I mean, really, aren't the fruit vendors going to suspect something if they see oranges and cantaloupes waltzing about in the middle of the road? Unless of course you only want to steal invisible fruit.

GRIFFIN. You're missing the point here, Millie. The point is that an invisible man can go places others cannot. He can see things others are forbidden to see.

MILLIE. Like what?

GRIFFIN. Like, oh, say, a beautiful young girl, bathing.

MILLIE. You want to be invisible so you can steal fruit and spy on women taking baths?

GRIFFIN. In a nutshell, yes.

(Pause.)

MILLIE. Have you spied on me?

GRIFFIN. Every chance I get.

MILLIE. No you haven't.

GRIFFIN. I'm afraid I have.

MILLIE. I don't believe you.

GRIFFIN. Do you mean you don't believe I would, or you don't believe I actually did?

MILLIE. I don't believe you ever had the opportunity. Besides, you've just been trying to convince me that you're blind.

GRIFFIN. I haven't been trying to convince you that I'm blind. I've been trying to demonstrate to you that you don't necessarily know if a person is blind or not, or invisible or not, unless you take the trouble to actually look at them, and then perhaps you still don't know.

MILLIE. I think you just like to say horrible things to people, tell ridiculous and filthy lies to people so you can feel superior to them.

GRIFFIN. You bathe yourself from a flowered wash basin in your ridiculously cramped, slope-eaved attic room by the gable window. Your breasts are pear shaped and very beautiful. The left one is just a bit larger than the right, but the assymetry is extremely arousing. Your pubic hair is quite full, and you have lovely dimples on your buttocks.

MILLIE. Who told you that?

GRIFFIN. Nobody told me that. I saw it for myself.

MILLIE. How did you see me? How could you possibly have seen me? Have you drilled yourself a peep hole in the walls?

GRIFFIN. Millie, pay attention. I'm invisible. Invisible. I crept into your room behind you as you closed the door. I stood a foot away from you, shivering there in your attic room. I was, of course, completely naked at the time.

MILLIE. Naked? You were naked in my room?

GRIFFIN. Well, I must go about naked, you see, or my clothing gives me the illusion of visibility.

MILLIE. I think I would have know if there was a naked man in my room, invisible or not.

GRIFFIN. Yes, you did look around once rather oddly, as if you had felt someone's breath upon the back of your neck. For a moment I had this terrible fear I had somehow become visible again. That would have been rather embarrassing for us both, wouldn't it? But you saw nothing. And then you began removing your clothing. And when you were quite naked you commenced bathing yourself.

MILLIE. Oh my God.

GRIFFIN. It was a kind of mystical experience for me. Not just the bathing, but the drying, and what came after.

MILLIE. Oh my God. You're lying. You're lying. You've made this up.

GRIFFIN. You caressed your nipples with your fingertips and gave a little moan. You ran your right hand down your stomach and place it carefully between your legs. You caressed yourself, looking into the mirror solemnly, almost tragically, as you did so. Then you lay down on the bed at an angle of perhaps ten degrees east of the perpendicular, and continued caressing your right nipple with your left hand, while moving the middle finger of your right hand deeper and deeper into your body, slowly moving your right index finger back and forth upon the little knob of flesh above the entrance to your vagina. You were moaning quietly, so as not to awaken the cross-eyed cook, who sleeps in the broom closet next door. You closed your eyes as you were moaning, then opened them wide again just before you brought things to a rather spectacular conclusion, your body writhing upwards like a serpent being decapitated by a garden hoe. Then you lay there for a bit, your hands still resting upon yourself, sobbing quietly on the bed. You kissed your forearm as if it were a lover. Then you slipped on your nightgown, put the candle out, and crept under the covers, where you lay for a long time in the moonlight, whispering to your invisible lover. I'm sorry to report that I was unable to make out exactly what you were saying. Then gradually you drifted off. When I was certain you were sleeping, I crept over and kissed you very tenderly and chastely upon the forehead and tucked the covers round you just a bit more tightly. Then I crept out of the room, carefully closing the door behind me. It was, I firmly believe, the most profound and possibly the only true religious experience of my life.

(Pause.)

MILLIE. What a monster you are.

GRIFFIN. Yes, Millie. I am a monster. I am the thing you fear most and desire most. I am the Bogey Man who waits at night to creep into your bed, but then in fact does not. I am the summation of all your childhood hopes and fears. I am your devoted imaginary lover. I am, in short, the Invisible Man.

MILLIE. Let me see.

GRIFFIN. Let you see what?

MILLIE. If you're invisible, let me see you.

GRIFFIN. Millie, I fear you have still not properly grasped the concept of invisibility.

MILLIE. Take off those bandages and let me see you.

GRIFFIN. But you won't be able to see me. I'm invisible.

MILLIE. I want to see the empty space where you would be if you were here.

GRIFFIN. Don't you believe? Don't you believe that I am invisible?

MILLIE. I want to see it.

GRIFFIN. You can't see it. That's what being invisible is all about. Do I have to draw you a picture in invisible ink?

MILLIE. I want to see that I can't see it.

GRIFFIN. What?

MILLIE. You've been looking at me, spying upon me.

GRIFFIN. I'm invisible. That's my job.

MILLIE. You've been creeping into my room like a rat at night and looking at me naked, looking at me washing myself naked, looking at me lying naked upon the bed. Well, now I want to look at you.

GRIFFIN. Ah, but you see, Millie, it is really very much like God with me.

MILLIE. God?

GRIFFIN. Yes.

MILLIE. Like God? You're like God?

GRIFFIN. Very like.

MILLIE. In what possible way could you be like God?

GRIFFIN. In my invisibility, of course. You must take it on faith that I am here, even though all you can see are a few foolish wrappings which clearly are not me at all. You must take it on faith. For if I should attempt to show myself to you, in all my grotesque invisible nakedness, then, like God, I would be revealed to you as nothing. As absolutely nothing. I would vanish, in short, entirely into thin air. You must believe without putting your fingers into my open wounds, so to speak, or I vanish entirely. So, do you believe, or don't you? *(Grasping her forearms in his hands and gazing into her eyes.)* Do you believe I am invisible? Do you believe that underneath these wrappings I am in fact nobody, I am in fact nothing, I am in fact entirely imaginary, as imaginary as the invisible person who comes to your room at night and comforts you and makes love to you through your fingertips when you are naked, as utterly and eternally unseeable, unknowable, inscrutable, sadistic and eternally invisible as the Lord God Almighty, Maker of Heaven and Earth, who cometh to judge the quick and the dead? Do you believe that or don't you?

(Pause. His face is very close to hers.)

MILLIE. Yes. I believe that.
GRIFFIN. Good. In that case, you are dismissed.

(Pause.)

MILLIE. I'm dismissed?
GRIFFIN. Yes. *(He lets go of her and turns away.)* You may go now. I am done with you. I require nothing more from you. I am content. The Invisible Man is content.

(Pause.)

MILLIE. All right.

(She stands there a moment looking at him, rubbing her arms where he held them. Then she turns to go.)

GRIFFIN. Millie?
MILLIE. Yes?
GRIFFIN. What about your secret?
MILLIE. My secret?
GRIFFIN. We've forgotten your secret.
MILLIE. What secret?
GRIFFIN. Don't you remember? We made a bargain. I said

I'd tell you my secret if you'd tell me yours. Well, I've told you my secret. Now you must tell me yours. You must keep your end of the bargain with the Invisible Man, Millie. I'm not letting you off the hook, here. So. Come on. Out with it. What's your secret?

MILLIE. I thought you already knew all my secrets.

GRIFFIN. Oh, no. Not at all. I have seen your flesh. I have seen you bathe your flesh by moonlight. I have watched you make love to your loneliness and your despair. But I don't know your secret. I still look at you, as it were, entirely from the outside. So, what is your secret, Millie? Tell me your secret. I should like very much to know your secret.

(Pause.)

MILLIE. My secret— *(Pause.)* My secret is that I am invisible, too.

(Pause.)

GRIFFIN. Yes. I can see that.

(Pause. They look at each other. The light fades on them and goes out. Just the ticking clock in the darkness.)

END OF PLAY

Other Publications For Your Interest

DOCTOR DEATH. (All Groups.) Thriller-Farce. Mark Chandler. 3m., 9f. (can also be 4m, 8f. or 5m., 7f., via two male or female roles) That pixilated playwright of merry murder is at it again: The author of the marvelous *I Shot My Rich Aunt* takes us this time to the French Riviera, on a pleasure yacht just off Cap d'Antibes, where the happy guests of a mysterious host discover they're all marked for a madman's murderous vengeance. Their first clue that this will be less than a pleasant outing arrives in a deck of Old Maid cards, in which each is named—and rather nastily described. And with this clue comes the horrifying realization that one of them is a cruel and calculating killer. But which one? Can the malevolent mastermind be lovely Linda Luscious, handsome Victor Valor, bartender Margarita Martini, steward Queenie Quill, TV hostess Wendy Windy, shy secretary Portia Peck, sleazy Ritchy Raunchy, private-eye Harry Hulk, math-expert Sibyl Service, wrestler Minnie Mountain, actress Fanny Flop, or aerobics advocate Jillian Jogger? They'd better find out soon, because just after they realize that none of them can swim a stroke, they learn that the yacht is slowly sinking! (And in shark-filled waters, to boot!) Can they unmask the fiend in their midst? Can they figure out how to get off the doomed ship without drowning—or worse—in the process? Thrill follows chill in this madcap melodrama of hideous revenge—and there are so many gut-busting laughs along the way that you'll lose count! We promise you, this is a highly unusual variation on the trapped-by-a killer genre. The setting, the characters, and the convoluted plot are all superbly fascinating—and absolutely hilarious. A wonderfully zany evening of fun!   **#674**

I SHOT MY RICH AUNT. (All Groups.) Comedy. Mark Chandler. 4m., 5f. This rollicking romp through the British aristocracy's environs is a melange of off-the-wall farce and near-murder mystery. Every role is a gem and a delight for the performers. Lady Valonia Wendrew is having a number of people come to weekend at her stately manor (a former castle with a weird history) on the occasion of her nephew Dustin's announcement of his engagement to Judy Blake. Unluckily, Dustin's former flame Vivian Rexford has arrived to find out why Dustin dumped her two months previously, and Judy's brother Bingo Blake lets Dustin talk him into going outside to shoot at some starlings, and Lord Henry Mayhew, the family solicitor, is coming to change Valonia's will *out* of Dustin's favor, and Judy's school chum Gwendolyn Natterly is coming to meet—and ensnare—Dustin's cousin Nigel, a humble curate who thinks he's only there to meet Dustin's fiancee, and during the starling-shoot a stray bullet enters the library, and Dustin enters to find Valonia with a small hole in her blouse surrounded by oozing warm red liquid, and by the time he's run and gotten Bingo to come in and help him know what to do, the aunt's body has vanished and Eloise the maid is suspected to Know All and is planning to blackmail Dustin and meantime the picketing cooks' and maidservants' unions have raised the estate's drawbridge, thus entrapping everyone as night falls, and then Henry's wife thinks he's having an affair with Gwendolyn and she arrives with horsewhip in hand on the incoming fire engine (did we tell you the place is on fire?) You're going to be sore from the endless belly-laughs, all the way to the utterly insane finale!   **#11103**

DEATH DEFYING ACTS
David Mamet • Elaine May • Woody Allen

"An elegant diversion."
N.Y. TIMES
"A wealth of laughter."
N.Y. NEWSDAY

This Off-Broadway hit features comedies by three masters of the genre. David Mamet's brilliant twenty-minute play INTERVIEW is a mystifying interrogation of a sleazy lawyer. In HOTLINE, a wildly funny forty-minute piece by Elaine May, a woman caller on a suicide hotline overwhelms a novice counselor. A psychiatrist has discovered that her husband is unfaithful in Woody Allen's hilarious hour-long second act, CENTRAL PARK WEST. 2 m., 3 f. (#6201)

MOON OVER BUFFALO
Ken Ludwig

"Hilarious ... comic invention,
running gags {and] ... absurdity."
N.Y. POST

A theatre in Buffalo in 1953 is the setting for this hilarious backstage farce by the author of LEND ME A TENOR. Carol Burnett and Philip Bosco starred on Broadway as married thespians to whom fate gives one more shot at stardom during a madcap matinee performance of PRIVATE LIVES - or is it CYRANO DE BERGERAC? 4 m., 4 f. (#17)

Samuel French, Inc.
SERVING THE THEATRICAL COMMUNITY SINCE 1830

CEMENTVILLE
by Jane Martin
Comedy
Little Theatre

(5m., 9f.) Int. The comic sensation of the 1991 Humana Festival at the
famed Actors Theatre of Louisville, this wildly funny new play by the
mysterious author of *Talking With* and *Vital Signs* is a brilliant portrayal of
America's fascination with fantasy entertainment, "the growth industry of
the 90's." We are in a run-down locker room in a seedy sports arena in
the Armpit of the Universe, "Cementville, Tennessee," with the scurviest
bunch of professional wrasslers you ever saw. This is decidedly a small-
time operation—not the big time you see on TV. The promoter, Bigman,
also appears in the show. He and his brother Eddie are the only men,
though; for the main attraction(s) are the "ladies." There's Tiger, who
comes with a big drinking problem and a small dog; Dani, who comes
with a large chip on her shoulder against Bigman, who owes all the girls
several weeks' pay; Lessa, an ex-Olympic shotputter with delusions that
she is actually employed presently in athletics; and Netty, an overweight
older woman who appears in the ring dressed in baggy pajamas, with her
hair in curlers, as the character "Pajama Mama." There is the eager-
beaver go-fer Nola, a teenager who dreams of someday entering the
glamorous world of pro wrestling herself. And then, there are the
Knockout Sisters, refugees from the Big Time but banned from it for
heavy-duty abuse of pharmaceuticals as well as having gotten arrested
in flagrante delicto with the Mayor of Los Angeles. They have just gotten
out of the slammer; but their indefatigable manager, Mother Crocker ("Of
the Auto-Repair Crockers") hopes to get them reinstated, if she can keep
them off the white powder. Bigman has hired the Knockout Sisters as
tonight's main attraction, and the fur really flies along with the sparks
when the other women find out about the Knockout Sisters. Bigman has
really got his hands full tonight. He's gotta get the girls to tear each other
up in the ring, not the locker room; he's gotta deal with tough-as-nails
Mother Crocker; he's gotta keep an arena full of tanked-up rubes from
tearing up the joint—and he's gotta solve the mystery of who bit off his
brother Eddie's dick last night.   (#5580)

✔✔✔✔✔✔✔✔✔✔✔✔✔✔✔✔✔✔✔✔✔✔✔✔✔✔✔✔

OTHER PUBLICATIONS FOR YOUR INTEREST

COASTAL DISTURBANCES
(Little Theatre- Comedy)

by TINA HOWE

3 male, 4 female

This new Broadway hit from the author of *PAINTING CHURCHES, MUSEUM,* and *THE ART OF DINING* is quite daring and experimental, in that it is *not* cynical or alienated about love and romance. This is an ensemble play about four generations of vacationers on a Massachusetts beach which focuses on a budding romance between a hunk of a lifeguard and a kooky young photographer. Structured as a series of vignettes taking place over the course of the summer, the play looks at love from all sides now. "A modern play about love that is, for once, actually about love--as opposed to sexual, social or marital politics . . . it generously illuminates the intimate landscape between men and women." --NY Times. "Enchanting."--New Yorker. #5755

APPROACHING ZANZIBAR
(Advanced Groups—Comedy)

by TINA HOWE

2 male, 4 female, 3 children --Various Ints. and Exts.

This new play by the author of *Painting Churches, Coastal Disturbances, Museum,* and *The Art of Dining* is about the cross-country journey of the Blossom family--Wallace and Charlotte and their two kids Turner and Pony--out west to visit Charlotte's aunt Olivia Childs in Taos, New Mexico. Aunt Olivia, a renowned environmental artist who creates enormous "sculptures" of hundreds of kites, is dying of cancer, and Charlotte wants to see her one last time. The family camps out along the way, having various adventures and meeting other relatives and strangers, until, eventually, they arrive in Taos, where Olivia is fading in and out of reality--or is she? Little Pony Blossom persuades the old lady to stand up and jump up and down on the bed, and we are left with final entrancing image of Aunt Olivia and Pony bouncing on the bed like a trampoline. Has a miracle occurred? "What pervades the shadow is Miss Howe's originality and purity of her dramatic imagination."--The New Yorker. #3140

New Comedies from
Samuel French, Inc.

THE LADY IN QUESTION (Little Theatre.-Comedy)
by Charles Busch.
5m., 4f. 1 int., 1 ext. w/insert.

This hilarious spoof of every trashy damsel-in-distress-vs.-the Nazis movie you ever saw packed them in Off Broadway, where the irrepressible Mr. Busch starred as Gertrude Garnet, world-renowned concert pianist and world-class hedonist. On tour in Bavaria, Gertrude finds her Nazi hosts charming; until, that is, she unwittingly becomes enlisted in a plot by Prof Erik Maxwell to free his mother, a famous actress who has appeared in an anti-Nazi play, from the clutches of the Fuhrer's fearsome minions. At first, Gertrude is more concerned about the whereabouts of her missing cosmetics bag; but when her best friend and travelling companion Kitty is murdered by the Nazi swine, Gertrude agrees to help Erik by manipulating the Nazi Baron Von Elsner, whose mansion becomes the escape route. Of course, Gertrude and Erik fall in love; and, of course, there is a desperate dash (on *skis,* no less!) to the safety of the Swiss border, where Gertrude and Erik find True Love. Mr. Busch's send-up of this film genre is so witty and well-constructed that, as the NY Times pointed out, it would be just as entertaining if the role of Gertrude were played by a woman. "Bewitchingly entertaining. I couldn't have had a better time, unless perhaps someone had given me popcorn."—N.Y. Post. "Hilarious."—N.Y. Times.
(#14182)

RED SCARE ON SUNSET (Advanced Groups-Comedy)
by Charles Busch.
5m., 3f. Unit set.

This Off-Broadway hit is set in 1950's Hollywood during the blacklist days. This is a hilarious comedy that touches on serious subjects by the author of *Vampire Lesbians of Sodom.* Mary Dale is a musical comedy star who discovers to her horror that her husband, her best friend, her director and houseboy are all mixed up in a communist plot to take over the movie industry. Among their goals is the dissolution of the star system! Mary's conversion from Rodeo Drive robot to McCarthy marauder who ultimately names names including her husband's makes for outrageous, thought provoking comedy. The climax is a wild dream sequence where Mary imagines she's Lady Godiva, the role in the musical she's currently filming. Both right and left are skewered in this comic melodrama. "You have to champion the ingenuity of Busch's writing which twirls twist upon twist and spins into comedy heaven."—Newsday.
(#19982)